Proceedings of the Third International Coach Federation

COACHING

RESEARCH

SYMPOSIUM

November 9, 2005
San Jose, California, USA

Edited by
Francine Campone and John L. Bennett

**International Coach
Federation**

A publication of the International Coach Federation
coachfederation.org

Published by International Coach Federation
2365 Harrodsburg Rd, Suite A 325
Lexington, KY 40504-3335

Publisher's Cataloging-in-Publication Data
International Coach Federation Coaching Research Symposium (3rd : 2005 : San Jose, Calif.)

Proceedings of the Third International Coach Federation Coaching Research Symposium : November 9, 2005, San Jose, California, USA / edited by Francine Campone and John L.
Bennett. – Lexington, KY : International Coach Federation, ©2006.

p. ; cm.
ISBN: 0-9758868-9-4
ISBN13: 978-0-9758868-9-2

1. Personal coaching—Congresses. 2. Self-actualization (Psychology)—Congresses. 3. Goal (Psychology)—Congresses. 4. Motivation (Psychology)—Congresses. I. Campone, Francine. II. Bennett, John L. III. Title.

BF637.P36 I58 2005
158.3-dc22   2005934649

Printed in the United States of America
09 08 07 06 05 • 5 4 3 2 1

Proceedings of the Third ICF Coaching Research Symposium

November 9, 2005 • San Jose, California

Poster Presenters' Papers

2005 White Papers

Message from the ICF President

Steve Mitten

It's a sad truth that, in our young and evolving profession, too few potential clients truly appreciate the value and power of a great coaching relationship.

It's also unfortunate that too few coaches truly appreciate the importance of a strong body of research in establishing a new profession.

To everyone involved in the conducting, discussing and reporting of research into the field of coaching, I want to extend my heartfelt gratitude. The work you do is vitally important to building a healthy and effective profession. I know of no other group that has greater potential to positively impact our evolving profession.

The ICF is committed to supporting and furthering research into the field of coaching. We are very proud to support the 2005 Coaching Research Symposium, which is only made possible through the tremendous efforts of a team of dedicated and hard-working volunteers. To everyone who has contributed to making this symposium a reality, thank you very much.

It is our great hope that through the efforts of the coaching research community, we will realize a much better future for all coaches and clients around the world.

Steve Mitten

Message from the ICF Research and Development Committee Chair

Don Morrow

The 2005 International Coach Federation Coaching Research Symposium is the third annual research symposium held under the auspices of the ICF. At the present time, the ICF reports that there are an estimated 10,000 part- and full-time coaches worldwide. Coaching itself is regarded as an art and a science. More specifically, in the words of the ICF, "Coaching is an interactive process that helps individuals and organizations to develop more rapidly and produce more satisfying results. As a result of coaching, clients set better goals, take more action, make better decisions, and more fully use their natural strengths." These are bold claims and as coaches, we all "know" that coaching works. What any profession must have is solid research to support its mandate. This Proceedings represents some of the research being done toward that imperative.

The Research and Development Committee is tremendously proud of the work being done by so many volunteers in order to make this year's symposium a success, and we want to acknowledge all of them for their commitment, professionalism, and goodwill. Mary Wayne Bush and her Organizing Team, Linda Page and her Program Team have been zealous and efficient in organizing the Symposium. Francine Campone and John Bennett and all of the referees selected to review papers and posters and panelists for the Symposium did a remarkable job. I would direct you to Francine's paper on "evolving a model of coaching research" and the whitepaper related to the 2004 Symposium by Linda Page and Irene Stein published in this volume. And to all of the researchers who have contributed to this Symposium and thereby to the coaching profession, thank you for your expertise and critical insights, conclusions, and directionality.

The Keynote speakers for all three of the symposia have made clarion calls for integrating coaching research with coaching practice. Indeed. We simply cannot have one without the other for the sake of coaching's future and for the sake of truly making a difference in the world. I envision and hold that there is room for all dimensions of coaching-related research from evidence-based to less rigorous but equally important styles of research. We do not need more independent "silos" of research ungrounded in a profession; nor do we need more hierarchical structures some of which are deemed to be somehow more important than others. Instead, we want integrative research that moves the profession forward just as coaching serves to move clients forward. Our vision is to truly partner research about coaching with the profession of coaching and we urge all of you to think and work inclusively to that end. We are on the threshold of possibilities for coaching and this Symposium is one more step toward the limitlessness of what coaching can do for humankind.

Don Morrow, Ph.D., CPCC, is a certified professional, co-active coach who is actively engaged both in his practice of life coaching and in doing research about coaching. Together with his wife Jennifer Irwin, Ph.D., CPCC, he runs his coaching business, Possibilities Life Coaching, and supervises graduate students who are pursuing research careers in coaching. Contact: dr.morrow@possibilitieslifecoaching.com.

Message from the Symposium Chair

Marywayne Bush

This year's theme for the ICF Coaching Research Symposium is Coaching Research: Building Dialogue. The aim of the Symposium organizers was to provide a forum for research-grounded conversations between and among academicians, coach researchers and practitioners, and individuals and groups engaged in coach training and education, to build a foundation for shared understanding.

The papers included in this volume represent several dimensions of this dialogue, and continue the precedent set by the previous two Symposia in sharing and promoting excellence in the coaching research field. The 2005 Symposium event encourages dialogue across several dimensions among constituent groups that have an interest in the future of coaching research. Coaching practitioners, researchers and educators are all involved in research on our field, and have valuable contributions to make in enriching our understanding of its philosophical and theoretical foundations, its models and practices, and its connections with other fields. A robust, rigorous dialogue about coaching and research has the power to help our profession become stronger, and to inform and empower coaches, educators and researchers alike.

This volume further extends the dialogue, inviting you — the reader — into the discussion across distance and time. I hope you will expand and build on what you read here, perhaps gaining ideas or perspectives for your own research on coaching. And I encourage you to reach out and contact the authors and Symposium organizers as well, to let us know what you are thinking.

Mary Wayne Bush, Ed. D. is a coach, consultant, author and educator. As an Organization Development Analyst at Lockheed Martin Space Systems in Sunnyvale, CA, she works with leaders and teams to improve operational effectiveness in the workplace. Her doctoral research on the effectiveness of executive coaching has been published and presented at national and international conferences. She teaches in the coaching certificate program at California State University, Long Beach, and has taught quality management courses for University of California, Santa Cruz Extension. Dr. Bush is a member of the Editorial Board of the International Journal of Coaching in Organizations (IJCO) and was co-editor of the 2005 issue on Perspectives in Coaching Research. She earned her Master's degree from Yale University and doctorate in Organizational Change from Pepperdine University. Contact marywayne.bush@lmco.com.

Introduction from the Editors

Francine Campone
John L. Bennett

The pages of this Proceedings of the 2005 International Coach Federation Research Symposium contain a World Café of research conversations. In reading these papers we enter the dialogue the authors are holding with colleagues. Listening more closely, we can hear the other voices in the room: the voices of other researchers, educators and practitioners, as well as those of their clients, whose thinking, responses and writings contribute to framing and supporting the authors' views.

All agree on this point: research is essential if coaching is to become a professional practice. In his keynote address, W. Barnett Pearce moves the conversation even further, noting that coaching is a profession, which not only impacts individual lives but has the potential to affect the human community as a whole by promoting and sustaining dialogue. Stober, Wildflower and Drake encourage coaches to consider a multifaceted conversation which integrates the voices of clients, researchers and the coach's own inner wisdom. Their evidence-based approach suggests (to at least one of us) that coaching can have the energy of a jazz improvisation, with the notes of coaching research and experience integrated into a unique response to the client's composition. Moore, Drake, Tschannen-Moran, Campone and Kaufman extend the musical dialogue with a theoretical model for an intuitive dance. Their paper suggests how the voices of researchers and theorists in four different arenas come together to form a state or field in which coach and client dialogue flows.

Elsewhere in our literal café, we find three-way conversations as the focus of research papers. Baldwin, Johnson, and Reding ask what affects a program of coaching skills for education leaders had on their participants. In drawing their conclusions, they listened not only to the voices of the program participants but also to the shared examples of coaching conversations the participants had with others. "Practitioner" takes on multiple meanings as Braham explores the impact of meditation practice on coaching practice. She extends the field of root disciplines in coaching to include the Dharma worldview and the inner dialogue practice of Vipassana meditation and engages in dialogue with her co-researchers to collaboratively explore the effects. Recognizing the interplay between coaching research, practice and education, Campone's whitepaper, Quantum Framework, suggests that coaching research be viewed in a way that acknowledges the interdependence of these relationships. The model, borrowed from the field of Physics, calls attention to the dance of certainty and uncertainty, static and dynamic, intimacy and distance.

While the full spectrum of participant voices explicit in many of the papers, some focus on a quieter exchange, that between coach and client. Crawshaw's consideration of ethics in coaching research listens to the voices of coach researchers and clients in equal measure. She brings her voice to the conversation with thoughtful recommendations for research practice. Maitland's paper allows the reader to eavesdrop on the conversations between peer coaches in South African companies. We hear clearly that these conversations have moved the participants to a deeper appreciation of others and the capacity to bridge differences. With an Adaptive Coaching model, Terry Bacon invites coaches to engage with clients in a way that is responsive and reflective of their needs, wants and characteristics. Orem, Clancy, and Binkert offer three case studies that show how the principles of Appreciative Inquiry can be used to amplify positive, client-centered coaching and promote constructive change for both coach and client. Client's voices are also clearly expressed in Creane's study of their perspectives on coaching. Her paper offers generous shares of the participants' own expressions, rich material for consideration by coaches and those involved in forming definitions within the field of coaching.

The three poster presenters bring all the voices back into the room. The Martins offer a model unifying multiple theories and practice. Kassel suggests avenues for coaching researchers and practitioners to explore collaboratively. Dingman voices client perspectives on coaching as a means of helping to resolve competing commitments. The White Paper by Page and Stein brings echoes of the panel discussion at the 2004 Research Symposium in which six participants offered their perspectives on coaching, evidence, coaching education and the evolution of a profession. Page and Stein enrich this dialogue with their own contributions and perspectives and invite the readers to continue the conversations as the 2005 Symposium takes place and in an ongoing way afterward.

We appreciate the depth, breadth, and diversity of the papers, the evidence and reflection offered by the authors, and the opportunity to add our voices. We cordially invite readers and Symposium participants to listen deeply, speak their own truths, and continue the conversations.

*Francine Campone, Ed.D., PCC served as a university counselor, faculty member and Associate Dean of Students over the course of a twenty-nine year career. She earned her doctorate in Higher and Adult Education from Columbia University. She earned the International Coach Federation's Professional Certified Coach (PCC) designation. Training in humanistic mediation, group dynamics and facilitation, and Constructive Living Practice complements her coach training. Francine works extensively with leaders of education and nonprofit organizations, and with individuals and teams facing in significant transitions. A founding faculty member of the School of Management's graduate coaching certification program at the University of Texas at Dallas, Francine developed and teaches a course in research for coaches. Dr. Campone was co-editor of the Proceedings of the 2004 ICF Research Symposium and is a member of the leadership team for the 2005 Symposium as well as co-editor of this year's Proceedings.
Contact: fcampone@rushmore.com.*

John L. Bennett, MPA, MA, PCC is a member of the organizational communication faculty at Queens University of Charlotte and is founder of Lawton Associates an executive coaching and management consulting firm based in Charlotte, NC. He is a founder of the ICF Research Symposium and past president of the Charlotte Area Chapter of the ICF and is a member of the leadership team for the 2005 Symposium as well as co-editor of this year's Proceedings. He is author of numerous articles and two books. Mr. Bennett earned a Master of Public Affairs degree from the University of North Carolina at Greensboro and a Master's degree from Fielding Graduate University where he is currently a doctoral candidate in human and organizational systems. He earned the International Coach Federation's Professional Certified Coach (PCC) designation. His current research interests focus on the influence of lived experience on the formation of scholarly work, leadership development, and the professionalization of coaching. Contact: bennettj@queens.edu.

Dialogue and Research in the Development of Coaching as a Profession

W. Barnett Pearce

> *Coaching is part of an emerging new sensibility about human relationships, and it is vital that this new sensibility evolve quickly. Rapid developments in technologies are putting unprecedented capabilities into human hands, and our collective fate depends on whether we use them well. To the extent that coaching is effective in developing this new sensibility and bringing it to key decision makers, society as a whole needs you to be successful in developing your profession.*
>
> *The form of communication in which you handle disagreements will do more to shape the development of coaching as a profession than the positions you take about specific issues. For these purposes, dialogic communication is better than the more common DAD (Decide-Advocate-Defend) pattern.*
>
> *Research is a powerful way of stimulating the development of coaching, and the role of research in the profession will determine the extent to which coaching drives the development of the new sensibility about relationships. I bring in three voices – Maslow, Gergen and Barrett – to help think about how we should understand research within the new sensibility, and another three voices – Rorty, Fairhurst and my own – as conversation partners in thinking about the kind of research that is needed.*
>
> *The differences and disagreements among those of us gathered for the Symposium is a vital asset. We can achieve personal learning and collective enrichment by engaging each other in dialogue, particularly those with whom we disagree the most.*

The theme of this Symposium is "Coaching Research: Building Dialogue." It is an honor to be invited to address a group summoned by those good words.

Coaching is Part of a New Sensibility About Human Relationships

We live in a time of rapid change. As a child, my grandmother rode an ox-cart when she and her family went into town; as a senior citizen, she watched the live televised broadcast of Neil Armstrong walking on the moon. These changes are giving us unprecedented capabilities, but they are not necessarily giving us the wisdom to know how to use them.

In many fields, the pace of change is exponential. The power of computers doubles every 18 months, the capacity of information storage and retrieval technology doubles every 12 months, and the bandwidth of the Internet doubles every nine months. We have every reason to believe that biogenetics and nanotechnology will create far greater differences in the span of a lifetime in the 21st century than my grandmother experienced in the 20th. Even in their saner moments, visionaries in both of these fields speak of virtual immortality, unlimited resources, and the ability to live in harmony with – or to destroy – the earth (Ratner and Ratner, 2003). In their darker moments, they refer to the

Singularity, when artificial intelligence will outstrip human ability to comprehend and predict (Retrieved June 26, 2005, from http://www.aleph.se/Trans/Words/s.html#SINGULARITY).

Fortunately, technology is not the only driver of change. There is also a new sensibility about human relationships that involves collaboration, cooperation, sustainability and dialogic communication. There is no single, agreed-upon way of describing this new sensibility. One suggestion is "civic maturity:" applying the tools used to assess the maturity of new computer software to describe social processes in a community (Pearce, 2001). I like the notion of "communicative virtuosity:" the ability to discern the differences among emerging patterns of communication and to act effectively in calling into being desirable patterns (Pearce, 2005). Yet another idea is that of "corporate integrity," in which it is the integrity of the organization collectively, not of individual members in the organization, that is of interest (Brown, 2005).

I have recently worked with mid-career doctoral students who are involved in coaching, mediation, therapy, mentoring, diversity training, and organizational development. While there are some interesting and important differences among these fields of practice, there are also some strong similarities.

One happy conclusion to draw is that you, as coaches, are not alone in working out new ideas and traditions of practice. You have opportunities for cross-fertilization of ideas, mutual support, and synchronous efforts. For marketing and brand-name purposes, it might be important to draw distinctions among coaching and these cognate fields, but for other good and useful purposes, you might better see them as kindred spirits and fellow-travelers.

Another conclusion to draw has to do with the stakes involved in your success. We are in a race between the development of this new sensibility and the other drivers of change and it is vitally important that this sensibility "wins." Speaking as one who is not a coach, I believe that your success as coaches is crucial to all of us.

Scenario-building operates by identifying the drivers for change and then imagining what happens depending on which drivers prevail (Hammond, 1998; Pearce, 2000). We know that the pace of technological development is going to be fast; imagine the consequences if the pace of the development of this new sensibility is fast or slow in comparison to that rate. If the drivers of technology outstrip the new sensibility, then crucial decisions are likely to be made people immersed in what Buber (1958) called I-it relationships with each other and with the environment, and using confrontational patterns of social interaction as their first resort. If this is what happens, the most likely scenarios are very dark.

On the other hand, if the pace of development of the new sensibility is fast in relationship to the other drivers, then the decisions about power, information, bio-engineering and nanotechnology are likely to be made in collaborative processes involving all stakeholders and by people in what Buber (1958) called I-thou relationships with those affected by the decisions. If this is what happens, then, just maybe, we might collectively make social worlds that we would want for our children and grandchildren.

Your clients are among those who will make the decisions about how to use the capabilities that new technologies will confer. What kind of resources will they bring to bear? To what extent will your work with them contribute to their wisdom in making these sorts of decisions as well as to their personal and professional development? Gonzáles' (2004, p. 97) found that the effects of coaching on coaches included "experiences of transformation." The coaches in her study described themselves as having "better relationships, different ways of being in the world, change of perspectives, personal transformation, self-acceptance, continuous learning, more curiosity, more awareness of self and others, and finding more meaning for their lives" (p. 97). If your clients have similar experiences, and are in position to make important decisions that will affect us all, then we have reason for hope and confidence.

The Importance of Dialogue in the Development of the Profession of Coaching

In the past few months, I have talked with a lot of coaches about coaching, and I have learned that you disagree about a lot of things. You bring different learning histories to your practice; you have different metaphors and models for coaching; you even disagree about the relative importance of coaching practice, research, training, and education.

These and other disagreements are to be expected in an organization as large and as young as this. The question is, how will you handle these disagreements? If you handle them well – in dialogic communication — they can function as vital assets, strengthening your profession and enriching each of you individually. I'm using a technical sense of "dialogue" here. I do not mean just talk; rather, I'm referring to a particular quality of communication in which you remain in the tension between standing your ground and being profoundly open to the other (Pearce and Pearce, 2004; Stein, 2004). If you treat them dialogically, disagreements call for more and better communication.

In dialogic communication, it makes sense to say, "We disagree? Wonderful! How did you come to hold your position?" Dialogic conversations enlarge perspectives rather than constrict them; enable us to discover more about our own positions than we had originally known; permit us to address the "gray areas" as well as the things about which we are certain; and, paradoxically, in the absence of the attempt to persuade, we often come to agree with each other.

But that's not the way we usually treat disagreements in our professional lives. Twenty-five years ago, I realized how much I tried to avoid disagreements. After attending the annual conference of the International Communication Association, I went to a conference for practitioners. As I met the therapist with whom I was leading a workshop, he asked where I had been. When I told him, he asked if it had been a good conference and I replied "yes." "Oh?" he said, "what did you learn?"

The question stunned me. The criteria by which I was accustomed to evaluate academic conventions depended on the extent to which I was able to move my own agenda forward. I would have felt comfortable with questions such as "Did your presentation go well?" and "Did you get to meet Professor X?" Learning from – not just about – other people and their work was not what I expected to do. Avoiding disagreements shuts us off from the possibility of dialogic communication. Dialogue is a way of being in relation to the other that makes "What did you learn?" an obvious question.

My own professional discipline was formed in patterns of communication that had little to do with dialogue, and we've paid a high price for it. For fifty years – from 1911 to the early 1960s — my discipline organized itself into competing and confrontational schools of thought. As it turned out, it did not matter which of these schools were right. While the careers of particular individuals waxed and waned, the discipline found itself in what I have learned to call DAD, or Decide-Advocate-Defend. Highly intelligent, articulate men and women decided which school was right, advocated it, and defended it against the attacks by the other. Among other things, this pattern of communication impeded progress in our thinking about communication, reduced our contributions to society, and made us vulnerable to the series of hostile takeovers by ideas and individuals from outside our discipline that started in the 1960s (Pearce, 1985).

As a communication theorist, I believe that patterns of communication are substantial and that we make the social worlds in which we live. That is, the primary questions are "what are we making together when we act this way?" and "how are we making it?" rather than "what position are we taking about the issue?" (Pearce, 2004). To the extent that this claim is correct, the form of communication in which you handle your disagreements will, more than the positions you take on the issues or who wins the arguments, shape the development of your profession.

Dialogic communication is the most radical alternative to the DAD model. In dialogue, individuals are called to listen, inquire, understand, explain, and find ways of moving forward together (see Stein, 2004). Disagreements and differences are seen as sites for mutual learning, not intellectual pugilism. The art of posing questions is valued at least as highly as that of expressing one's own opinions. The narrative forms of self-disclosure and inquiry are more highly prized than that of advocacy. Had my discipline used this form of communication, it would have developed more quickly and more robustly and would have made a much greater contribution to the world.

The Role of Research in Helping Coaching Reach Its Full Potential

The keynote speakers in both of the previous Symposiums endorsed a "scientist-practitioner model" for members of your profession (Grant, 2004; Stober, 2005). I am not sure that they meant exactly the same thing by that term, and this is one possible site of difference around which dialogue might occur. But I want to raise at least two other issues. If coaching is a part of a new sensibility about human relationships, a sensibility that includes terms like civic maturity, communicative virtuosity, and corporate integrity, 1) how should you understand research, and 2) what kinds of research should you do?

How Should You Understand Research?
The new sensibility of which coaching is a part is itself part of a new paradigm in research methods and the philosophy of science. The older paradigm of research rested on three assumptions, that researchers: 1) can and should describe reality as it is without subjective distortion; 2) can and should leave the world as it is because their role is to

study it, not intervene in it; and, 3) can and should seek general relationships among well-defined variables. Above all, research "must be...rigorous and ...demanding, and it must clearly differentiate established fact and advocacy" (Lowman, 2005, p. 95).

As a former practitioner within it, I think that this is a fair characterization of the old paradigm. And let me point out that it is also an exceptionally clear description of what Buber (1958) would call an I-it, or non-dialogical relationship between the researcher and the objects of study.

Some of us fault this paradigm because we think that we cannot act as it prescribes; others because we think that, even if we could, we should not. But even if we were to agree that research is something other than a dispassionate, objective description of law-like relations among operationally-defined variables, what similarly precise definition, more consistent with the new sensibility, might we use to replace it? That is, when you describe yourselves individually or your profession collectively as "scientist-practitioners, how should you understand what you are doing when you do research and/or use research in your work?

I do not have a good answer to this question, so let me move the conversation along by bringing in three additional voices: Maslow, Gergen, and Barrett. In The Psychology of Science, Abraham Maslow (1966, pp. 102-118) contrasted the old paradigm with what he described as "interpersonal (I-Thou) knowledge." He proposed a "law of learning and cognizing: Do you want to know? Then care!" (p. 104). Maslow said that research "can be meaningfully called an act of love." The minimum demand of research is "patience, stubbornness, stick-to-it-iveness, unswerving concentration on the task, the fortitude to over-come inevitable disappointments, etc." But "what is really needed for long-time scientific success is passion, fascination, obsession" (p. 110). Science, in Maslow's sense, is sacred.

> This is what nonscientists don't know, and this is what scientists are too bashful to talk about publicly, at least until they grow old enough to become shameless. Science at its highest level is ultimately the organization of, the systematic pursuit of, and the enjoyment of wonder, awe, and mystery... Science can be the religion of the nonreligious, the poetry of the nonpoet ... Not only does science begin in wonder; it also ends in wonder (Maslow, 1966, p. 151).

Speaking in Maslow's language: do you love coaching enough to study it in this way? Are you sufficiently filled with wonder, awe and mystery to stick to it? Are you so deeply involved that it becomes the aesthetic expression of your soul as well as a way of collecting nuggets of information?

Ken Gergen (1973) noted that every research study is located in the language and situation in which it is done. As such, the findings of research are "history" rather than invariant laws of the universe. Building on this premise, he argued that research should be "generative" rather than pretending to describe things as they are, self-consciously building the world in which we live rather than pretending to leave the world as it is (Gergen, 1978). The function of those of us who seek knowledge is "transformation" (Gergen, 1994).

...during the past century the sociobehavioral sciences have participated in one of humankind's greatest intellectual adventures. They have...joined in the "pursuit of the incorrigible," or certain knowledge, a pursuit that has challenged thinkers from Heraclitus to the present. Early in this century, it appeared that the means had been discovered for gaining certainty in the behavioral sciences. Yet subsequent examination has found such means sadly wanting. The search for certainty is a child's romance, and like most, one holds fast to even the most fragile shard attesting to continued life. The question that must now be confronted is how to pass successfully into the maturity of a second century. A new romance is required to extinguish the old, and it appears that the overtures are at hand (p. 209).

Speaking in Gergen's voice: are you mature enough in your philosophy of science to lay aside the notions of an unerring method for producing "truth"? If so, are you creative enough to develop or find methods appropriate for research that makes the world that it studies? Are you sufficiently self-aware to engage in research responsibly, knowing that we all can and should be transformed by your findings?

Frank Barrett (in press) suggests that we should apply to our research a premise from appreciative inquiry: what we pay attention to, grows.

By creating linguistic categories, distinctions and causal attributions, scientists are publicly defining reality, guiding people by shaping the way they talk about life, how they report their own and others' experiences, indeed, how people actually have experiences. It would be very unlikely for a 19th century woman to describe herself as "codependent," for example. Such labels for reporting and noticing behaviors did not exist. The contention here is that it is not intrinsic human nature that has changed; rather it is the language we use to talk about human experiences that has changed and social scientists help to create what is taken to be normal and legitimate. Further, a limited set of inferences for actions flow from these theoretical terms, influencing who we are and what we are able to become for one another. Once a linguistic repertoire of "codependency" and its family resemblances becomes accepted, a new set of actions becomes possible such as the formation of support groups, therapy that encourages women to separate from domineering husbands, etc. Many of these actions were much less imaginable 40 years ago...

...Perhaps social scientists should try to formulate interesting and provocative hypotheses, to challenge the limitation of current problem solving, to stretch beyond safety, even if conventional evidence eventually renders these theories less useful. A new language may emerge, one that provides a conceptual scaffold, a way to talk about the ineffable potentials of human experience that our old safe language not only fails to grasp, but does not even attempt to articulate. Perhaps such searches may make possible a bolder, more appreciative view of human action, a probing into the innovative potential of human behavior.

Since theorists are in the business of creating language, research efforts can be poetic acts, efforts to forge new words that grapple with the seemingly in expressible potential of human action. Social research can become an exhilarating adventure: rather than conservative efforts to solve existing problems, social research can involve bold, courageous efforts, an openness to discovering new questions, a move to rekindle fresh perception of the ordinary. Research, like poetry, if it is going to have a profound impact on the social world, assumes a stance of wonderment and questioning in regards to unfathomable, dimly perceivable mysteries. Like poets, we can assume a stance of awe and fascination; we can question the spectacles that surround us under guise of ordinary, everyday life; attempt to articulate the vaguely sensed, to illuminate notions that energize, inspire, move people in ways that vitalize rather than bore; provide new conceptual schemes for others to ponder; transfer words from familiar domains into areas where they do not belong, thus altering the contours of both domains.

Speaking in Barrett's voice: are you sufficiently poetic in your research? Are your hypotheses sufficiently interesting, provocative, and bold? Does your research break through the limits of conventional thinking so that it has the potential of forging new perspectives and better ways of life?

What Kinds of Research Should You Do?

When I was in graduate school, the question was whether to do research or not. My students now face the much more complicated question of what kind of research shall they do? Empirical-descriptive? Hermeneutic-interpretive? Critical? Action research? And not only do each of these categories have a dozen or so specific variants within them, they have different criteria for evaluating the conduct and results of that research.

Many of us have discovered that paradigms are both real and different when we submitted research papers to journals for peer review. Perhaps some of you have had the experience of having your work rejected when the reviewers applied the evaluative criteria of one paradigm to a study done in another. Reading those rejection letters is a bitter lesson that what counts as a good argument and an exciting finding in one paradigm sounds like quite something else in the other (Fairhurst, 2000; Chen and Pearce, 1995).

In the new sensibility, our research has to serve two, not necessarily compatible functions. Because the future of our planet depends on the rapid evolution of the new sensibility, we need to do research that is passionate, provocative and generates new forms of life. And yet, because it is also important that the new sensibility include those not already committed to it, we must do research that is credible to those who would hold up other standards, including those of the old paradigm. How do we do both? Let me bring in three voices: Rorty, Fairhurst, and my own.

Richard Rorty (1979, p. 58) said, "Bad arguments for brilliant hunches must necessarily precede the normalization of a new vocabulary which incorporates the hunch. Given that new vocabulary, better arguments become possible..." If I understand him, Rorty suggests that we ask "for whom is this research intended." That is, some of the research that we do might not seem very innovative or feed the passions of those already in the new sensibility, but it is both credible and persuasive to those who are not – and whose support we need.

Gail Fairhurst (2000) coined the term "paradigm crossing" to describe the situation many of us find ourselves in when submitting our work for publication or describing it to potential clients or colleagues. As she points out in her example of an award-winning article that was rejected by the first journal to which it was submitted, any attempt to address those outside one's own paradigm has the potential for generating controversy. She offers practical advice about how to avoid the common triggers of the "paradigm skirmishes" that occur in the private correspondence between author, editor and peer reviewers, and concludes that we have to be "willing to skirmish…the review process is an opportunity for cross-paradigm learning for reviewers as well. As the authors' mistakes are revealed, so too are the reviewers' assumptions, biases, and lack of knowledge made known" (pp. 126-7).

We can drive ourselves crazy by forgetting where we are in our paradigm crossings. I have seen researchers use a new method to explore a creative question and then, once the data is in, seek to meet all the criteria of the old paradigm in which neither that method nor that question could have been framed.

See the tension? Because of the necessity of what Rorty (1979) called "bad arguments for brilliant hunches" that legitimize us in the eyes of those in the old paradigm, we must cross paradigms, but when we do, we risk confusing ourselves and driving ourselves crazy.

I do not think that this tension can be resolved; it has to be lived with. And to live in this tension successfully, it helps to know what we are doing. And I know of no better way for us, individually or collectively, to know what we are doing than to engage in dialogue.

Conclusion

The fact that our individuality is forged in social relationships, and that we come to know ourselves best when in conversation with a good listener, is part of the new sensibility. Paradoxically and wonderfully, the best way for us to remember where we are when we do paradigm crossing in our research, or to find ways of move forward together as a profession, comes when we seek out and engage in dialogic communication those who disagree with us the most. We learn about them and about ourselves when we invite them to tell us how they came to hold the positions that they do, and what would be the consequences in their lives if they were to give up those positions. And if we do that, while simultaneously responding to their invitations to us, we will find ourselves saying things we did not expect to say and perhaps did not know that we knew.

Fortunately, we have in this room many people who disagree with you and whose experience differs from yours. That is, people from whom you can learn. At the end of this day, may you have a good answer to the questions that my friend put to me:

Was it a good conference?

Yes!

Oh? What did you learn?

References

Barrett, F. J. (in press). *A value free conception of science. International Encyclopedia of Organizational Studies.* Thousand Oaks, CA: Sage.

Brown, M. T. (2005). *Corporate integrity: Rethinking organizational ethics and leadership.* New York, NY: Cambridge University Press.

Buber, M. (1958). *I and thou* (2nd ed.). New York, NY: Charles Scribner's Sons.

Chen, V. & Pearce, W. B. (1995). Even if a thing of beauty, can a case study be a joy forever?" In W. Leeds-Hurwitz (Ed.), *Social approaches to communication* (pp. 135-154). New York, NY: Guilford.

Fairhurst, G. T. (2000). Paradigm skirmishes in the review process. In S. R. Corman & M. S. Poole (Eds.), *Perspectives on organizational communication: Finding common ground.* (pp. 120-127). New York, NY: Guilford Press.

Grant, A. M. (2004). Keeping up with the cheese! Research as a foundation for professional coaching of the future. In I. F. Stein & L. A. Belsten (Eds.), *Proceedings of the First ICF Coaching Research Symposium* (pp. 1-19). Mooresville, NC: Paw Print Press.

Gergen, K. J. (1974). Social psychology as history. *Journal of Personality and Social Psychology, 26:* 309-320.

Gergen, K. J. (1978). Toward generative social theory. *Journal of Personality and Social Psychology, 36:* 1344-1360.

Gergen, K. J. (1994). *Toward transformation in social knowledge* (2nd ed.). Thousand Oaks, CA: Sage.

Gonzáles, A. L. (2004). Transformative conversations: Executive coaches and business leaders in dialogical collaboration for growth. In I. F. Stein & L. A. Belsten (Eds.), *Proceedings of the First ICF Coaching Research Symposium* (pp. 94-103). Mooresville, NC: Paw Print Press.

Hammond, A. (1998). *Which world? Scenarios for the 21st century.* Washington, DC: Shearwater Books.

Lowman, R. L. (2005). Executive coaching: The road to Dodoville needs paving with more than good assumptions. *Consulting Psychology Journal: Practice and Research, 57:* 90-96.

Maslow, A. (1966). *The psychology of science: A reconnaissance.* South Bend, IN: Gateway.

Pearce, W. B. (1985). Scientific research methods in communication studies and their implications for theory and knowledge. In T. Benson (Ed.). *Speech communication in the twentieth century* (pp. 255-281). Carbondale, IL: Southern Illinois University Press.

Pearce, W. B. (2000, October). Reflections on the role of "dialogic communication" in changing the world. Paper presented to Change and Development at the Turn of the Millennium, Rhodes, Greece. Available at http://www.pearceassociates.com/essays/essays_menu.htm

Pearce, W. B. (2001, July). Civic maturity: Musings about a metaphor. Paper presented to the Action Research Symposium, Fielding Graduate Institute, Alexandria, Virginia.
   Available at http://www.pearceassociates.com/essays/civic_maturity.htm

Pearce, W. B. (2004). The coordinated management of meaning (CMM). In W. Gudykundst (Ed.) *Theorizing about intercultural communication* (pp. 35-54). Thousand Oaks, CA: Sage.

Pearce, W. B. (2005, April). Toward communicative virtuosity. Paper presented to Modernity as a communication process (Is modernity 'on time.' Russian State University for Humanities, Moscow, Russia.
   Available at http://www.pearceassociates.com/essays/essays_menu.htm

Pearce, W. B. & Pearce, K. A. (2004). Taking a communication perspective on dialogue. In R.Anderson, L. A. Baxter, & K. N. Cissna (Eds.) *Dialogue: Theorizing difference in communication studies* (pp. 39-56). Thousand Oaks, CA: Sage.

Ratner, M. & Ratner, D. (2003). *Nanotechnology: A gentle introduction to the next big idea.* Upper Saddle River, NJ: Prentice Hall.

Rorty, R. (1979). *Philosophy and the mirror of nature.* Princeton, N.J.: Princeton University Press.

Stein, I. F. (2004). The "coach-approach" as dialogic discourse. In I. F. Stein & L. A. Belsten (Eds.). *Proceedings of the First ICF Coaching Research Symposium* (pp. 130-139). Mooresville, NC: Paw Print Press.

Stober, D. R. (2005). Coaching eye for the research guy and research eye for the coaching guy: 20/20 vision for coaching through the scientist-practitioner model. In I.F. Stein, F. Campone, & L. J. Page (Eds.), *Proceedings of the Second ICF Coaching Research Symposium* (pp. 13-21). Washington, DC: International Coach Federation.

 *Barnett Pearce, Ph.D. is Professor in the doctoral program in the School of Human and Organization Development at Fielding Graduate University, having previously served as Department Chair at Loyola University Chicago and the University of Massachusetts at Amherst. A communication theorist, Dr. Pearce is one of the primary developers of the theory of "coordinated management of meaning". His research is closely connected to practice, and vice versa. He is a founding member of the nonprofit Public Dialogue Consortium and co-Principal of the for-profit Pearce Associates. Among other things, he is the recipient of three awards from his academic discipline for scholarship, was appointed as a Fulbright Scholar to Argentina, and was a Senior Visiting Scholar at Linacre College, Oxford University. He has published seven books and over 100 chapters and articles. Contact: bpearce@fielding.edu.*

Ethical Considerations in Qualitative Coaching Research

Laura A. Crawshaw

Research on coaching is in its very early stages. The International Coaching Federation's Coaching Research Symposium, first convened in 2003, is a positive indicator of the discipline's commitment to researching coaching practices. Like psychotherapy, coaching is most often a process conducted between two people – coach and client – behind the closed doors of confidentiality. Coaching researchers have a responsibility to ensure that the social and psychological well-being of research participants is not adversely affected by the research. This paper addresses four issues in ethical research with human subjects: (a)complications arising from dual roles in research with past, current, and prospective clients; (b) issues of informed consent; (c)the handling of sensitive material; and (d)the potential for coercion. The paper concludes with a recommendation for the development and codification of ethical principles of coaching research.

Research into the practice of coaching is ethically necessary to ensure that the techniques applied are based upon solid evidence rather than speculation. This ethic holds for the fields of medicine, nursing, and psychology (McLeod, 1994), professions that continually seek to research and substantiate best practices. The emerging practice of coaching has yet to achieve the status of a true profession; to achieve the status of a respected profession, coaching practice must be built on a foundation of careful research (Grant, 2003).

Dual Roles in Practice and Research: Coach and Researcher

Is it ethical to conduct research on your clients? In the case of qualitative narrative research, is it ethical to submit the content of clients' confidential sessions to the scrutiny of your research interests? What are the ethical implications of simultaneously taking the role of coach, for the client's interests, and researcher, for your own interests?

To consider the ethics of conducting research with coaching clients it is helpful to look at other disciplines that engage in research on recipients of care: medicine, nursing, and psychology. The U.S. Department of Social and Health Services, in its Ethical Principles And Guidelines For The Protection Of Human Subjects Of Research (National Commission for the Protection of Human Subjects of Biomedical and Behavioral Research, 1979), also known as The Belmont Report, specifies that research may be conducted by care practitioners: "Research and practice may be carried on together when research is designed to evaluate the safety and efficacy of a therapy" (p.4). The Guidelines also specify that any research involving recipients of care should undergo review for the protection of human subjects. The American Psychological Association's (APA, 2002) Ethical Principles of Psychologists and Code of Conduct also condones the dual relationship of researcher and practitioner, emphasizing the need to protect individuals who choose to decline or withdraw from participation: "When psychologists conduct research with clients/patients, students, or subordinates as participants, psychologists take steps to protect the prospective participants from adverse consequences of declining or withdrawing from participation" (Section 8.04).

Grafanaki (1996) described the complications of conducting qualitative research on patients of psychotherapy where the researcher is also the therapist, noting that dual roles and role boundaries can create potential tensions between the researcher's role as interviewer and therapist's role as practitioner: "Although the researcher may provide information, reassurance and emotional support to the participants at some point during the research process, the major role is that of an investigator interested in gaining understanding about a particular phenomenon" (p. 335). He added that it is no easy task for the researcher to make clear the role boundaries between investigator and therapist, "especially when highly emotionally-charged material is shared, unresolved issues are revealed, and advice is sought" (p. 335).

Dual Roles in Research with Current, Former, and Prospective Clients

The role boundaries become extremely complex for the practitioner who conducts research concurrently with therapy or coaching, for in those situations the therapist's or coach's primary duty of pursuing the client's best interests may conflict with the researcher's priority of meeting the aims of the research study (Hart, 1999). The client may wonder whether a question is being asked to further the client's progress or to support the practitioner-researcher's theory. "Can I trust my coach's interventions, or am I just the guinea pig in an experiment? What if I don't follow my coach's recommendations? Will my coach become resentful because it could ruin the research? Will my coach be disappointed in me if I decide not to participate, and feel less committed to my coaching process?" The practitioner contemplating research with current clients needs to possess the expertise to manage the oftentimes-conflicting priorities of practice and research described in this paper. A coach who cannot competently manage the competing agendas of concurrent practice and research —for which there are currently no specific guidelines (Richards and Schwartz, 2002) —may not ethically expect the client to grapple with the potential anxieties of working with a coach who is in a dual role

In the case of qualitative research into the content of coaching sessions, it is preferable, if the research design allows, to devote one's focus entirely to the client's needs while coaching, without concern for the requirements of a credible research process and without burdening the client with the additional anxieties of being a research participant. Sole focus on coaching guarantees that the client's needs take precedence. Research can proceed once the coaching process has concluded, allowing the needs of the coaching client and coaching researcher to be addressed sequentially. While this may require a greater timeframe for research, the accomplished practitioner often has the opportunity to draw upon former clients' case studies for research rather than attempting to manage the delicate balance of dual or conflicting roles with current clients.

Etherington (1996) noted that research with former clients may bear the further advantage of a previously established relationship of trust developed in the course of providing care. A third advantage lies in previous knowledge of the client that can inform the appropriateness of the decision to involve that client in research. Another advantage in conducting research on former clients can be found in the fact that the material to be studied is complete and finite. When deciding to submit one's experience to research, the former client-prospective participant can review a static document and fully excise any information deemed sensitive. These advantages do not exist when researching current or prospective clients.

The conducting the processes of coaching and research sequentially rather than concurrently permits participants to determine at each phase whether they wish to engage in the specific demands of the given process. This is not to say that research cannot be conducted concurrently with coaching. Wosket (1999) stated that such research conducted sensitively and ethically by therapists, far from being damaging or exploitative, can actually serve to enhance the therapeutic experience of clients by allowing a reciprocal relationship where each party works to enhance the quality of the therapy. A similar advantage may exist in sequential, post-coaching research in that the former client is given a new opportunity to reflect upon and refine insights gained from the coaching experience, benefiting both client and researcher.

When conducting research and coaching concurrently, the research design should not interfere with achievement of the client's coaching goals. Any potential for interference, despite the coach-researcher's best efforts to avoid such a situation, should be discussed immediately at the moment of recognition. The client should then be given the option to withdraw from participation in research without negative consequences for their coaching process. If the coach-researcher clearly sees that continuing research will obstruct pursuit of the client's goals or best interests, the research should be abandoned in support of the client's progress.

Finally, the research design should be clearly explained to the client, including the rationale for research. The coach-researcher should encourage clients to discuss any concerns they have regarding participation in the processes of coaching and research, including the abovementioned competing agendas of coach-researcher and client-participant. Even if the client expresses minimal or no concern, the coach-researcher should address potential anxieties and reassure the client regarding the coach's assumption of the dual roles of coach and researcher.

Informed Consent

One could argue that using former clients in research is more ethical, in that the participant is fully cognizant of the sensitive information they revealed in the course of coaching before giving consent for research. However, even if participants in qualitative studies have prior knowledge of the contents of their coaching sessions, the potential exists that negative information may emerge in responses given to subsequent questions asked as part of the research study. Ethical research with former, current, or prospective clients requires that clients from any timeframe have full control of determining exactly what sensitive information will be included in the research.

Coaching incorporates many of the techniques of qualitative research — specifically, generation and analysis of narratives — to gain information regarding the client's history, attitudes, and behavior. Like coaching, "Qualitative research aims at an in-depth under-standing of an issue, including an exploration of the reasons and context for participants' beliefs and actions, so is often designed to be probing in nature" (Richards & Schwartz, 2002, p. 136). The authors cited interviewing as the most common qualitative method in health services research, noting that it is particularly well suited to the collection of data on sensitive topics.

The ethics of seeking consent to use private information applies to all qualitative research approaches that analyze the text of respondents' discourse on personally significant experiences (Knapik, 2002). Such research, often referred to as narrative-type research (NTR), explores texts of human experience (Polkinghorne, 1988). In the conversation-like interviews of NTR, the researcher is actively working to elicit private information (Cowles, 1988).

Etherington (1996) pointed out that in narrative-type research the participants are asked to share aspects of their experience relevant to the topic at hand. The same holds true for coaching, where the coach asks the client to explore experiences relevant to the client's goals. "These interviews may be very unstructured. The emergent nature of NTR means that participants cannot be told in detail what they will experience. Consequently, traditional ethical guidelines of informed consent to prevent harm did not transfer well to new approaches" (Knapik, 2002, p. 4).

Thus, in narrative research on the contents of a therapy or coaching process, current and prospective clients who are about to participate in a research process cannot truly give informed consent at the outset of the study, because what may emerge or be revealed in their coaching work cannot yet be known. Further, if a client were to consent to concurrent research and coaching, one could argue that the participant has the opportunity and perhaps the burden to self-censor, thereby withholding sensitive information from the researcher's investigative lens. In such cases the client, for fear of being subjected to the scrutiny of research, may risk depriving the coach of information and interaction that may have benefited the client's coaching process.

Conversely, Richards and Schwartz (2002) cautioned that participants in concurrent research may divulge more information than they had anticipated when originally consenting to the study. Other researchers have voiced concern that participants may reveal things that they later decide are too sensitive to report (Cowles, 1988). In their meta-analysis of psychotherapy research outcome studies, Smith and Galss (1977) admonished researchers to be aware that despite a person's agreement to take part in a study, it cannot be known for certain what the interviews will uncover. One response to this concern is the practice of ongoing informed consent, *or process consent.*

Process Consent

There is general agreement among health care researchers (Richards & Schwartz, 2002; Smythe & Murray, 2000) that traditional principles of research ethics provide insufficient guidance on the issue of the intrusive and interpretive nature of narrative inquiry. Richards and Schwartz (2002) stated that few articles about qualitative methods in health services research have dealt with ethical issues, and those that have addressed the issue have been published primarily in nursing journals.

There are two approaches to securing participant consent in qualitative research. Traditionally, participants have been asked to give very general consent at the beginning of the study. Richards and Schwartz discourage this practice, instead recommending that the researcher treat consent as an ongoing process rather than a one-time event. The concept of process consent was developed in response to the difficulty of determining the potential harm and benefit of research participation. The British Sociological Association's Statement of Ethical Principles (2002) stresses the desirability of involving participants in decisions taken at all stages of the research process and suggests that consent should not be regarded as "a once-and-for-all prior event but as a process, subject to renegotiation over time" (Section 25, p. 3). The British Sociological Association Statement notes that the principle of involving participants in the planning, implementation, and dissemination of research is long established in sociology, and is increasingly recognized by the academic medical community and funding bodies.

With this approach, informed consent takes the form of process consent, also known as *ongoing renewed consent* (Munhall, 1988). Process consent requires the researcher to assess consent throughout the course of the research project, thereby giving the participant full authority to limit the use of sensitive information at any stage (Grafanaki, 1996). In this interpretation, consent is conceptualized as "a verb, a process, with the ethical components constantly being scrutinized" (Munhall, 1988, p. 161).

Grafanaki (1996) called for the researcher to continuously assess, through feedback, not only the handling of sensitive information, but also the impact of the research procedures on the participant, changing any parts of the inquiry process that create discomfort. The responsibility of initiating and securing continued consent lies with the researcher (Smythe & Murray, 2000). "Only in monitoring the impact of participation throughout the research process, and renegotiating consent, can the emergent nature of the research process be accompanied by responsible caring" (Knapik, 2002, p.8). Unlike a single request for consent prior to initiation of research, process consent gives the participant, whether a former or future client, the power to prevent the use of sensitive information at any point in the research process. The practice of process consent might also enrich the coaching experience, providing recurring opportunities to reflect upon the process, outcomes, and potential meanings of that experience, as well as enhancing the research process by enlisting the ongoing input and involvement of client-participants as co-researchers.

Handling Sensitive Information

In the disciplines of medicine, nursing, psychology, and coaching —of which, at this point, only the first three are recognized as scholarly (Grant, 2003)—a key question arises: how should the researcher handle sensitive (e.g., negative or distressing) material encountered in the course of research? This question leads to the issue of how to treat sensitive client information in the research process. Hart (1999) pointed out similarities between interviewing in therapy and qualitative research:

> In both there is a telling of experiences by one participant, while the other listens with a view to making sense, interpreting, reframing and understanding the narrative. In fact, if one were to eavesdrop on such an interaction, could one tell the difference between a therapy session and a research interview? (p. 205)

As any coach knows, exploration of sensitive topics may provoke anxiety or distress in participants; this anxiety may well be magnified by the prospect of allowing access to this information in a research process. The coaching or research questions that evoke emotional distress depend entirely on the individual's experience; neither coach nor researcher should presume to accurately predict what material the participant will perceive to be sensitive or negative.

As a coach and researcher of abrasive executives, I am well acquainted with the anxieties related to confidentiality experienced by this population at the prospect of participating in research: "Will people be able to identify me as a participant? Will I be associated with negative information regarding my past behavior? Will my organization find out, with repercussions for my future employability? How can I be sure that information I consider very private won't be written up for public consumption?"

To protect against threats to participant confidentiality and anonymity, the following procedures should be followed, discussed with prospective participants, and included in the informed-consent documents:

- All identifying information will be kept confidential and anonymous; the client and coach-researcher will be the only persons who know of the client's participation in the study.
- Participants will be asked to review the researcher's data sources – notes, transcripts, etc. – regarding the client, prior to inclusion of this material in the research process. The client-participant should sign a separate form giving consent to use this material.
- Participants will have the right to request that any information they consider sensitive and wish to keep private not be used in the research.
- Names, titles, positions, employers, industries, locations, and any other potentially identifiable participant information will not be used or will be altered to protect the participant's anonymity without distorting the demographics of the research; participants will be identified by pseudonyms only.

- No individual apart from the researcher or approved research assistants will have access to confidential material.
- Confidential materials will be stored in a manner that prevents access by other than approved research personnel.

Such procedures will protect participants' anonymity and provide important details in their consideration of informed consent.

Coercion: Compelling Clients to Participate

The National Commission for the Protection of Human Subjects of Biomedical and Behavioral Research (1979) defined coercion in research.

> An agreement to participate in research constitutes a valid consent only if voluntarily given. This element of informed consent requires conditions free of coercion and undue influence. Coercion occurs when an overt threat of harm is intentionally presented by one person to another in order to obtain compliance (p. 8).

The American Psychological Association (APA) adopted this exact language in defining coercion in its 2002 Ethical Principles of Psychologists and Codes of Conduct. Examples of coercion include the threat of revealing identifying information if the individual refuses to consent to participate, withholding access to further professional services, or exerting influence to negatively impact the individual's situation. A more subtle form of coercion consists of threatening disapproval or denigration of the patient's judgment should they choose to decline participation. Richards and Schwartz (2002) suggested that when a researcher is also a care provider, participants may feel pressured to participate in research because of a sense of duty to the practitioner, or because they depend on the good will of their service provider. To prevent the possibility or perception of coercion, they caution the practitioner-researcher to be clear and explicit with the former client-potential participant about role boundaries.

It is assumed that no responsible coach-researcher would intentionally engage in coercion However, to guard against the potential for unintended perceptions of coercion, the coach-researcher should carefully analyze each step of the proposed research process for the possibility that the client, despite the researcher's best intentions, might feel compelled to participate. This is best achieved through empathy: putting one's self in the prospective participant's shoes to explore potential perceptions of the research process. The client may feel compelled to participate because of a perceived obligation to please the coach, or the client may fear that the coach will react with resentment and reduced commitment to the coaching process should the client decline involvement in the research.

To assure that former, current, or prospective clients considering involvement in research do not feel coerced, however unintentionally, to consent to research participation, their potential anxieties should be explored and clients should be informed of the following before their written consent to participate is requested:

- It is perfectly understandable if the client chooses to decline participation, as many individuals involved in confidential processes such as coaching may not wish to participate in research, and involvement in a research process inevitably entails a burden upon a participant's time.
- The client's decision to accept or decline participation will be held in strict confidence; no other person will be informed of the request to participate.
  The choice to accept or decline participation in the research process will in no way affect the coach's availability or commitment to the client.

Careful consideration of client's experience of the proposed research process from the client's point of view will help the coaching researcher assess and manage the potential for perceptions of coercion.

Conclusions

Research on coaching is in its very early stages (Grant, 2003); the International Coaching Federation's Coaching Research Symposium (Stein and Belsten, 2003), first convened in 2003, is a positive indicator of the discipline's commitment to researching coaching practices. Like psychotherapy, coaching is most often a process conducted between two people, coach and client, behind the closed doors of confidentiality. Because of this, coaches have a responsibility to determine best practices through the promotion of research, and coach-researchers have a responsibility to safeguard the interests of client-participants.

Coach-researchers have a responsibility to ensure that the social and psychological well-being of research participants is not adversely affected by their research, and should be aware of their nation's laws and ethical standards in related professions that could affect their conduct of research on human subjects. Protecting the rights and securing the duly informed consent of research participants demands vigilance in assessing the potential for conflicting interests of dual roles, for coercion, and for the unauthorized use of sensitive material.

As the practice of coaching evolves into a profession founded upon reflexive scholarly research and theoretically informed praxis, the time has come to codify ethical principles for coaching researchers. Engaging in thoughtful discourse and documenting the most effective and humanistic ways to conduct research with our clients cannot help but contribute to the ethical pursuit of coaching research that will advance the progress of clients, researchers, and the profession.

References

American Psychological Association. (2002). *Ethical principles of psychologists and code of conduct.*: Washington, DC: American Psychological Association.

British Sociological Association. (2002). *Statement of ethical practice for the British Sociological Association.* Durham, England: British Sociological Association.

Cowles, K. V. (1988). Issues in qualitative research on sensitive topics. *Western Journal of Nursing Research, 10,* 163-179.

Etherington, K. (1996). The counsellor as researcher: Boundary issues and critical dilemmas. *British Journal of Guidance Counselling, 29,* 5-19.

Grafanaki, S. (1996). How research can change the researcher: the need for sensitivity, flexibility and ethical boundaries in conducting qualitative research in counselling/psychotherapy. *British Journal of Guidance and Counselling, 24,* 329-338.

Grant, A. M. (2004). Keeping up with the cheese again! Research as a foundation for professional coaching of the future. In I. F. Stein & L. A. Belsten (Eds.), *Proceedings of the First International Coach Federation Coaching Research Symposium.* Mooresville, NC: Paw Print Press.

Hart, N. (1999). Research as therapy, therapy as research: Ethical dilemmas in new-paradigm research. *British Journal of Guidance and Counselling, 27,* 205-215.

Knapik, M. (2002). Linking research to educational practice II. Paper presented at the Centre for Leadership in Learning Conference, Calgary, Alberta.

McLeod, J. (1994). *Doing counselling research.* London: Sage.

Munhall, P. (1988). Ethical considerations in qualitative research. *Western Journal of Nursing Research, 10,* 150-162.

National Commission for the Protection of Human Subjects of Biomedical and Behavioral Research. (1979). *Ethical principles and guidelines for the protection of human subjects of research.* Washington, DC: US Department of Health, Education, and Welfare.

Polkinghorne, D. E. (1988). Narrative knowing and the human sciences. Albany, NY: State University of New York Press.

Richards, H. M., & Schwartz, L. J. (2002). Ethics of qualitative research: Are there special issues for health services research? *Family Practice, 19,* 135-139.

Smith, M. L., & Galss, G. V. (1977). Meta-analysis of psychotherapy outcome studies. *American Psychologist, 32,* 165-180.

Smythe, W. E., & Murray, M. J. (2000). Owning the story: Ethical considerations in narrative research. *Ethics & Behavior, 10*(4), 311-337.

Stein, I. F. & Belsten, L. A. (Eds.) (2003). *Proceedings of the First International Coach Federation Coaching Research Symposium.* Washington, DC: International Coach Federation

Wosket, V. (1999). *The therapeutic use of self: Counselling, practice, research and supervision.* London: Routledge.

Laura Crawshaw, Ph.D., is founder and president of Executive Insight Development Group, Inc. The firm specializes in coaching abrasive executives and dysfunctional teams from a psychodynamic perspective. Originally a psychotherapist, Dr. Crawshaw has twenty years' experience as a corporate officer and clinical practitioner, and has served an international clientele of over 600 corporations. Her primary mission is the reduction of suffering in the workplace. Dr. Crawshaw received her master's degree in clinical social work from the Smith College School for Social Work and conducted postgraduate studies at the Seattle Institute for Psychoanalysis and Harvard Community Health Plan. She completed a second master's degree and doctorate in Human and Organizational Systems at Fielding Graduate University. She is a member of the International Society for the Psychoanalytic Study of Organizations and the International Coach Federation Research Council. Contact: crawshaw@executiveinsight.com.

Coaching Skills for Educational Leaders: Professional Development Experiences in One Public School District

Janet Baldwin Anderson

Katherine Johnson

Peter Reding

Twenty educational leaders volunteered to participate in the ten-month long program, Coaching Skills for Educational Leaders. The program, based on the International Coach Federation's coaching core competencies and the Inspired Learning Model™ principles, uses the The Standards of Presence ground rules as a tool to create a learning culture of trust, openness, and safety. The program included: (a) an initial four-day session to introduce and teach coaching skills; (b) teleclasses to reinforce skills and learning; (c) practice sessions with peer coaches; (d) a mid-year seminar; (e) practice in coaching offered by participants; and (f) an end-of-year seminar with presentations of "projects of excellence."

The research study evaluated the extent to which the program produced improvements in the coaching skills of participants. By developing new measures of self-reported proficiencies in coaching competencies, the study sought to demonstrate methods for quantifying participants' levels of coaching skill and for assessing changes in skill levels over time. Behavioral reports provided qualitative information about how participants applied the skills they learned in their schools.

The study found a significant increase in participants' self-reported proficiency in coaching skills over the ten-month program, as measured by the Coaching Skills Proficiency Survey (CSPS). In August 2004, participants' average self-rating on a seven point Likert scale indicated Moderate Proficiency. In January, the average rating indicated Moderately High Proficiency, while in May the average rating indicated nearly a High Proficiency level. The change in average proficiency ratings from August 2004 to May 2005 represented an increase of one and a half levels in proficiency. The study's findings suggest not only that participants strongly valued their experience with the program, but that they also demonstrated a greater sense of mastery and confidence in their use of coaching skills.

For the past three years, a county-wide public school system in Maryland has offered leadership development programs that included providing one-on-one professional coaching for educational leaders to develop their capacity to promote success for all students. Encouraged by the success of its professional coaching for leadership program, the school system undertook a more recent initiative in August 2004 to sponsor a school-year-long program for interested educational leaders, offering them the opportunity to learn coaching skills to use in schools.

A team of master coaches and Certified Inspired Learning Facilitators™ designed the ten-month professional development course, Coaching Skills for Educational Leaders. Based on the International Coach Federation's (ICF) coaching core competencies (www.coachfederation.org) and the Inspired Learning Model™ principles (www.inspiredlearning.org), the course emphasized the use of The Standards of Presence ground rules, one element of the Inspired Learning Model™. These ground rules served a tool to create a learning culture of trust, openness, and safety that sought to build participants' capacity to: (a) use coaching skills as leaders, (b) create positive learning environments, (c) become proficient in exploring cultural diversity, (d) foster student success by empowering the people they work with, and (e) manage challenging conversations.

The Coaching Skills for Educational Leaders program, taught entirely with the Inspired Learning Model™, incorporated ICF core coaching competencies as subject matter for the Inspired Learning Model™ approach. The Program included the following components: (a) an initial four-day session in the summer of 2004 to introduce and teach coaching skills; (b) two days of training in January 2005; (c) five teleclasses (two per month) from September through May to reinforce skills and learning; (d) twenty-four coaching practice sessions with peer coaches (three per month); (e) practice in coaching from January through May 2005, offered by participants to their staff or clients in schools and offices, with coaching facilitator support; and (f) a two-day end-of-year seminar in May 2005 with presentations of "projects of excellence."

As the professional development training was funded primarily through Title II federal funds for school improvement, an external evaluation researcher, contracted by the school system to provide consultation to the program, collected data throughout the year to measure program results. The aims of the professional development program were broad, for example, developing participants' ability to stay the course, remain engaged, not drop out, and take risks; apply new coaching and leadership skills on the job; integrate the learning into their leadership roles through projects of excellence; and shift attitudes from "what is not working" toward a focus on "what is working." The research focus addressed a more narrow goal, due to limitations of resources.

The research study evaluated the extent to which the program produced improvements in the coaching skills of educational leaders. It addressed the research question: "Did participants' coaching skills improve as a result of the program?" [H_0: no change; H_1: competencies improved]. The study aimed to break new ground by demonstrating a method for quantifying the level of self-reported change in coaching proficiency and performance over time.

Qualitative information also was obtained to provide behavioral report evidence for a secondary research question: "Do participants' apply the skills they learned in their schools?" Measures, described below, were developed specifically to address these two research questions and provide evidence of the program's impacts on the coaching skills of educational leaders. This report summarizes these efforts.

Review of Literature

Various theories and perspectives inform the approaches to coaching, leadership development, and learning applied in the Coaching Skills for Educational Leaders Program. Chief among these is a new learning theory based on the Inspired Learning Model, which fosters a positive learning environment that facilitates self-discovery and celebration of each step towards mastery. Other theories and perspectives are also relevant to these approaches. Adult learning (Knowles, 1975) is described as a process in which individuals diagnose their own learning needs, formulate learning goals, identify the needed resources for learning, choose and implement appropriate learning strategies, and evaluate their learning outcomes. Organizational learning (Senge, 1990) requires the development of five capabilities, or disciplines—systems thinking, personal mastery, mental models, building shared vision, and team learning—to create a learning organization. Emotional intelligence (Goleman, 1995) refers to social and emotional competence needed to motivate oneself and persist in the face of frustrations, to control impulse and delay gratification, and to empathize with others.

Guskey (1995) noted that there is little agreement among experts and researchers about how to implement successful professional development programs and argued (2000) that professional development must be an intentional, ongoing, and systemic process, with clearly stated goals, involving continuous learning both by the individual and by the organization. Guskey's (2000) five-level evaluation model provides guidelines for sustained evaluation activities.

A series of recent studies evaluating the effectiveness of the professional development programs in the schools (Porter, Birman, Garet, Desimone, and Yoon, 2004) identified a number of characteristics of effective professional development activities: sustained and intensive professional development, collective participation of groups of teachers, coherence of professional development activities that link with teachers' other experiences, and active learning opportunities. All are related to improvements in teacher knowledge and skill and changes in classroom practice (p.35).

The results of the current study will inform the knowledge base for coaching by providing an in-depth empirical example of the development of coaching skills through a professional development program in a public school district.

Method

Sample

Twenty educational leaders from a public school district in Maryland volunteered to participate in the program, Coaching Skills for Educational Leaders. This group, the target audience for professional development, forms a relatively homogeneous purposive sample. While more than half of the participants had experienced coaching from a certified coach for at least 6 months prior to the program, the rest were new to coaching. Therefore, the sample of senior educational leaders had varying degrees of familiarity with coaching. Four were male, 16 were female; two were African American, one was Asian, and 17 were Caucasian. Participants consisted of three principals; eight assistant principals; seven professional development facilitators; and two others (a resource teacher and a grants facilitator). All participants shared an interest in developing their coaching skills and a belief that coaching skills would improve their ability to communicate, support their professional learning, and increase their effectiveness as a leader in the workplace.

Instruments

Three measures informed the key research question: "Did participants coaching skills improve as a result of the program?" Each instrument was reviewed by four senior and/or ICF certified coaches and Certified Inspired Learning Facilitators. Revisions were made based on their comments. These measures included:

1. The Guskey Evaluation Form is a series of open-ended questions about what the participant would like to acknowledge in the following areas: the current professional development experience; the entire professional development experience; greatest learning; organizational supports that were present; what learning will be used; and what results have been observed for oneself, staff, and students; comments and suggestions.

2. The Coaching Skills Proficiency Survey (CSPS) is a newly-developed quantitative self-report measure of proficiency in each of eight core ICF coaching competencies. The paper and pencil survey was administered in person and collected at the initial session, the mid-term seminar, and the end of the program. The CSPS is a multiple item additive scale with items derived from selected ICF Core Competencies. The coaching core competencies assessed are creating trust, coming present and connecting, following the client's agenda, listening, asking powerful questions, acknowledging, creating awareness, and forwarding the learning.

These competencies also reflect concepts contained in the Inspired Learning Model's Standards of Presence, such as: maintain confidentiality, connect at a heart level, practice a positive focus, listen deeply, give authentic feedback, be open to acknowledgment, and be fully present. Thus, the CSPS has a high degree of content validity as an indicator of key aspects of the professional development program's content. The CSPS, which demonstrated excellent internal consistency (alpha = .95), employed a seven-point Likert-type scale to measure proficiencies from a low of 1(Beginner), to a high of 7 (Master). The definitions of these proficiency levels are presented in Table 1.

3. Pivotal Event Report Form (PERF) is a newly-developed qualitative protocol for systematically collecting participants' narratives describing behaviors associated with their coaching experience. The PERF was sent to and received from participants electronically. Adapted from the critical incident technique developed by John C. Flanagan (1954), the PERF is a formal qualitative methodology that includes three pieces of information: (a) a description of the situation that led to the incident, (b) the actions or behaviors of theprogram participant in the incident, and (c) the results or outcome of those actions.

This technique is useful for understanding the performance of individuals, systems, and organizations and for analyzing complex jobs in which the performance addresses

Table 1.
Seven Levels of Proficiency in Coaching Core Competencies from the
Coaching Skills Proficiency Survey
©2004 Janet Baldwin Anderson, Ph.D.

Ratings. The ratings below describe approximately equally spaced points on a 7 point Likert scale, where 1 indicates the <u>lowest level</u> of the rating and 7 indicates the <u>highest level</u> of the rating.

1. Beginner	Indicates an interest in the skill without proficiency.
2. Very Limited Proficiency	Indicates the barest beginning level of proficiency in the skill. Performance is limited to occasional demonstrations of the competency under very limited and carefully structured conditions, circumstances, or settings.
3. Limited Proficiency	Indicates a developing ability to demonstrate the skill under a limited range of conditions, circumstances, or settings but not yet at a consistent level of performance.
4. Moderate Proficiency	Indicates an ability to demonstrate the skill consistently under moderately varied conditions, circumstances, or settings.
5. Moderately High Proficiency	Indicates a moderately high ability to demonstrate the skill consistently under varied conditions, circumstances, or settings.
6. High Proficiency	Indicates a high ability to demonstrate the skill consistently under a wide range of conditions, circumstances, or settings.
7. Master	Indicates a very high ability to demonstrate a complete mastery of the skill consistently under all conditions, circumstances, or settings.

situations for which there is no immediately obvious solution. The PERF asked participants to describe an experience or an event in which they used or observed coaching skills in their work. Participants were asked to provide the basic details of the event (the situation), describe the behaviors of the main actors (actions), and indicate the outcome of those actions (outcome). They also were asked to identify relevant coaching competencies and suggest factors related to student learning.

Procedures

Based on the professional development evaluation methods of Thomas Guskey (2002, 2000, 1997), information was gathered at four of Guskey's five levels: (a) participants' satisfaction, (b) participants' level of learning, (c) organizational support, and (d) participants' use of their new knowledge and skills on the job. While no direct measures were obtained about the fifth level, student learning outcomes, participants were asked to report their perceptions about the impact of their coaching skills on student learning.

The study used observational and descriptive procedures in a quasi-experimental one-group pre-test, post-test design. Quantitative and qualitative data were collected at the beginning, middle, and end of the ten-month-long program. In August 2004, January 2005, and May 2005 each participant completed an evaluation form and a Coaching Skills Proficiency Survey. In addition, participants were invited to complete four Pivotal Event Reports, two per semester, using the form provided. Although no participant provided four, nearly half provided three reports. In light of how busy school leaders are during the crush of school year activities, the number of reports received seems acceptable and provides sufficient data to identify key themes about participants' experiences using coaching skills in their schools.

Some of the methodological limitations of the study should be noted. The use of a small, self-selected sample limits the generalizability of the results. The study cannot be said to demonstrate causal impacts of the professional development program or of the coaching models on which the program was based. To make any claim of causality would require an experimental design with a control group, often not feasible in field-based studies. Finally, the lack of known available measures for assessing change in coaching performance required the researchers to develop new qualitative and quantitative measures suited to the purposes of the study. Though these measures rely on self reported behavior and self-assessment of skills, they are appropriate as measures of participants' self-perceptions. However, as such measures are subject to response set bias, these results should be interpreted with caution.

Results

The program began in August of 2004 and ended in May of 2005. Results are presented for August 2004, January 2005, and May 2005.

Guskey Evaluation Forms

Based on evaluation comments from the initial, mid-point and final seminars, participants' level of interest and enthusiasm for a program that emphasized coaching, Inspired Learning, and cultural diversity were high at the start and remained positive through the completion of the Program. Participants acknowledged the program staff for their knowledge, skills, and openness; for creating a trusting, welcoming, and safe learning environment; for providing opportunity to practice coaching skills; and excellent planning and coordination. Specific comments emphasized the value of seeing coaching skills modeled by experienced coaches, having group discussions about cultural diversity, and using the Standards of Presence in their schools.

Coaching Skills Proficiency Survey (CSPS)

Proficiency ratings from the CSPS were analyzed using the Statistical Program for the Social Sciences (SPSS). Descriptive statistics and significance test results are presented in Table 2.

All participants responded to all items on the CSPS at all three points in time. Thus, there were no missing data. The average rating (and variance) for the seven point Likert scale was 4.3 (.20) in August 2004, indicating an overall Moderate Proficiency level of

Table 2.
Summary Statistics for <u>Coaching Skills Proficiency Survey</u>
(CSPS)

Overall Scale	Aug-04	Jan-05	May-05
Sample Size	20	20	20
Number of Variables	8	8	8
8 Variables - Mean	4.3	5.2	5.8
8 Variables - Minimum	3.8	4.9	5.4
8 Variables - Maximum	5.1	5.8	6.2
Average Variances	0.20	0.11	0.06
Individual Competencies			
Creating Trust	5.1	5.7*	5.9
Coming Present and Connecting	4.6	5.3*	5.7**
Following Individual's Agenda	4.2	5.3**	5.7**
Listening	4.7	5.8**	6.0**
Asking Powerful Questions	4.0	5.1**	5.8**
Acknowledging	4.5	5.2*	6.2**
Creating Awareness	4.0	4.9**	5.4**
Forwarding the Learning	3.8	4.9**	5.6**

<u>Note</u>: Significance tests compared average ratings in January 2005
with results in August 2004, and results in May 2005 with results
in August 2004, by competency.
*$p < .05$. ** $< .01$.

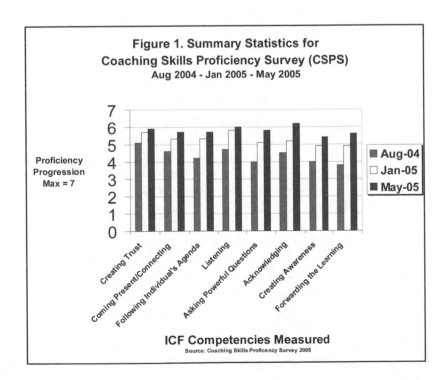

Figure 1. Summary Statistics for Coaching Skills Proficiency Survey (CSPS)
Aug 2004 - Jan 2005 - May 2005

Source: Coaching Skills Proficency Survey 2005

coaching competency; 5.2 (.11) in January 2005, indicating a Moderately High Proficiency level; and 5.8 (.06) in May 2005, approaching a High Proficiency level. Over time, not only do the ratings increase, but the variability in the ratings declines, suggesting either greater integration of skills as participants progressed in the program, or the ceiling effects due to more ratings clustering at the high end of the scale, or both.

As shown in Figure 1, participants' self-reported proficiency levels on the eight individual competencies ranged from Moderate to Moderately High Proficiency in August 2004, and increased in range from Moderately High to High Proficiency levels by May 2005. Comparisons between self-ratings in August 2004 and May 2005 were highly significant (p < .01) for all competencies but one, Creating Trust. In August 2004, participants' ratings were higher for Creating Trust (5.1) than for any other competency and by May 2005, these had increased to 5.9, a change of nearly one level. It is possible that with a larger sample, this change would have been found to be significant. Ratings on the other seven competencies increased by more than one level: Coming Present and Connecting (4.6 to 5.7), Following the Individual's Agenda (4.2 to 5.7), Listening (4.7 to 6.0), Asking Powerful Questions (4.0 to 5.8), Acknowledgment (4.5 to 6.2), Creating Awareness (4.0 to 5.4), and Forwarding the Learning (3.8 to 5.6).

These results, combined with the Guskey evaluation comments, suggest that respondents strongly valued their experience with the program, and they reported a growing sense of mastery and self-confidence in using their coaching skills.

Pivotal Events Reports

As of May 2005, 18 participants had provided at least one usable Pivotal Event Report, 14 had provided two, and 8 had completed three, for a total of 40 reports. Two participants did not provide a pivotal event report. Based on their narratives of a Pivotal Event related to coaching in schools, educational leaders identified the coaching core competencies related to the event and indicated their views about the implications for student learning. The content of the 40 reports were analyzed for their references to the ICF coaching competencies, settings, participants, and outcomes discussed.

Coaching Competencies. Among the 40 Pivotal Events reported, most described behaviors that demonstrated the competencies of Asking Powerful Questions (30 reports), Deep Listening (28), Creating Trust (23), and Acknowledging (22). Other coaching competencies described less frequently were Forwarding the Learning (18), Following the Individual's Agenda (16), Creating Awareness (16), and Coming Present and Connecting (10). The use of the Standards of Presence was mentioned in six of pivotal events.

Settings. Most of the coaching conversations (32 of 40) took place in meetings, such as committee meetings, staff meetings, teacher team meetings, parent meetings, IEP meetings, or one-on-one meetings. Settings for other Pivotal Events were classrooms (7) and administrator offices (2).

Participants. The most frequently cited people involved in the Pivotal Events were Principals and Assistant Principals (32) and Teachers (31). The next most cited participants were in a category comprised of Mentors, Professional Development Facilitators, and Central Office Staff (19). Students (9) and Parents (7) also were featured, but less often.

Outcomes. Most of the participants' analyses of their Pivotal Events suggested outcomes of coaching that positively affected students (29), teachers (29), or teams of teachers or mentors (17).

Key themes that emerged from the Pivotal Event Reports are:

1. Educational leaders applied the coaching skills they learned to coaching conversations that took place in meetings, primarily with teachers and staff.

2. These coaching conversations addressed a variety of situations and included a variety of participants (teachers, administrators, parents, and students).

3. Participants expected student learning to improve as a result of their use of coaching skills. The route to improved student learning includes fostering improvements in school climate, facilitating better relationships among teachers and instructional teams, helping teachers improve the content of their instruction, creating more coherent instruction, reducing student referrals, strengthening teachers' problem solving skills, creating safer more nurturing environments, and improving the emotional well being of teachers and instructional teams. There were some examples of participants whose coaching conversations influenced student behavior directly but most of the anticipated influence was through educational leaders coaching the school's teachers and staff.

Selected Edited Examples of Pivotal Event Reports

Example 1. Coaching a student. An assistant principal utilized the coaching skills of Acknowledging, Asking Powerful Questions, Making Requests to Forward the Learning, and Listening when talking with a new fifth grade student with a history of behavioral problems. The conversation enabled the student to change from acting out (hiding under the desk, leaving class, and being disrespectful) to deciding to return and apologize to the teacher and the class. As a result, the student acquired an increased sense of belonging to the class, pride, self-respect, and greater motivation for learning.

Participant's comment: "Coaching skills are invaluable for administrators and mentor teachers in making [students and] staff members feel empowered."

Implications for student learning: Since the event, the sense of pride acquired through this process of self-reflection greatly improved the student's motivation for learning.

Example 2. Coaching teachers. An assistant principal utilized the coaching skills of Listening and Asking Powerful Questions with a team of elementary school teachers meeting to discuss a student—below grade level in reading and mathematics—who entertains other students to avoid working and is disrespectful to adults. The teaching team at this school tended to solve their problems by asking for outside assistance. When the teachers suggested that the student be sent to the office and disciplined, the assistant principal listened some, asked some questions, and then asked a powerful question that made the difference: "What can you do to keep the child on the team, remove the child from the immediate attention getting situation, and allow the child to complete assigned work?" The teachers considered this. Then one suggested sending the child to a place where all teachers on the team could see the child. The child would be isolated from an audience, and they could ensure the student was doing the work. The outcome has been a great improvement from the daily referrals to the office.

Participant's comment: "The thing that made this powerful for me was that I knew I needed to step up and ask the question and I was able to do so quickly."

Implications for student learning: the team is handling an issue itself and doing it well.

Example 3. Coaching with a Colleague. An elementary school principle invited an experienced resource teacher to observe a kindergartner whose parents wanted the child accelerated to first grade and to share observations and recommendations at the team meeting with the parents. Though the child's classroom teacher and parents felt the child should be accelerated, the principal did not. The resource teacher utilized the coaching skills of Following the Individual's Agenda, Listening, Asking Powerful Questions, Acknowledging, and Creating Awareness to help foster a change in the principal's attitudes and assumptions about skipping a kindergarten child ahead to first grade. The resource teacher listened to all parties involved and presented alternative information for their consideration, while following the agendas of those involved. By fostering greater awareness on the part of the principal, the resource teacher encouraged a decision to accelerate the child.

Participant's comment: "Educational leaders in the system need to be coached or coach their staff on designing through empowerment the best possible solutions for problems that affect student and staff learning."

Implications for student learning: recognizing a student's advanced ability, challenging ability through acceleration, recognizing parental influences and support, considering data from formal and informal assessments, and respecting teacher recommendations.

Discussion

This study sought to contribute to the knowledge base for both the coaching field and professional development by describing how one group of educational leaders learned to use the ICF core coaching competencies, how these skills were measured over time, and what the participants reported about their experiences.

Schools increasingly are seen as places to help develop children's social and emotional competence, to fill the gaps when their families are unable to do so. Schools help students to become more tolerant, manage anger without fighting, handle stress, and show greater sensitivity to others' feelings (Goleman, 1995). According to Goleman (1995), programs designed to help students manage their emotions and increase their social and emotional competence have been found to improve children's academic achievement scores and school performance. Educational leaders' use of coaching skills helps to foster greater reflection, confidence, self awareness, sense of acceptance, and feelings of empowerment among teachers, school staff, and even parents—qualities that better enable them to do their jobs.

Having reliable and valid measures of coaching competencies will provide an important contribution to the advancement of coaching as a professional field. Preliminary results from this study found a high degree of internal consistency and reliability for the CSPS. It is recommended that the CSPS, along with other measures of coaching skills, be applied in larger and broader segments of the coaching community—from novice learners to master coaches, from educational leaders to executive leaders as well as coach trainees—to validate the use of these measures in other populations.

Educational leaders in the Maryland program reported significant increases in proficiency in their coaching competencies following ten months of coaching professional development. It is not known whether educational leaders less familiar with coaching would have achieved similar results. To extend the findings from this study into new areas, it is recommended that similar studies be undertaken with broader, more diverse, samples of educational leaders and with teachers. A longitudinal study, though more costly, is well worth considering as a way to evaluate the longer-term impacts of coaching in the schools and on student learning. Based on the positive response educational leaders have given to this Program, and the preliminary results from this study, the application of coaching skills as professional development appears to have considerable value in school settings.

References

Flanagan, J. C. (1954). The critical incident technique. *Psychological Bulletin, 41,* 237-358.

Foundation for inspired learning. Inspired Learning Model™. Retrieved September 6, 2005 from http://www.inspiredlearning.org/ILM.htm.

Goleman, D. (1995). *Emotional intelligence: Why it can matter more than IQ.* New York, NY: Bantam.

Guskey, T. R. (1995). Results oriented professional development: In search of an optimal mix of effective practices. Retrieved September 6, 2005 from www.ncrel.org/sdrs/areas/rpl_esys/pdlitrev.htm.

Guskey, T. R. (1997). Research needs to link professional development and student learning. *Journal of Staff Development, 18(*20), 36-40.

Guskey, T. R. (2000). *Evaluating professional development.* Thousand Oaks, CA: Corwin Press.

Guskey, T. R. (2002). Does it make a difference? Evaluating professional development. *Educational Leadership, 59* (6), 45-51.

International Coach Federation. Coaching core competencies. Retrieved September 6, 2005 from http://www.coachfederation.org/credentialing/en/core.asp

Knowles, M. S. (1975). *Self-directed learning: A guide for learners and teachers.* Englewood Cliffs, NJ: Prentice Hall/Cambridge.

Porter, A. C., Birman, B. F., Garet, M. S., Desimone, L. M., & Yoon, K. S. (2004). *Effective professional development in mathematics and science: Lessons from evaluation of the Eisenhower Program.* Washington, DC: American Institutes for Research.

Senge, P. M. (1990). *The fifth discipline: The art and practice of the learning organization.* New York, NY: Doubleday/Currency.

Statistical Program for the Social Sciences, SPSS. Chicago, IL.

Janet Baldwin Anderson, Ph.D., has over twenty years experience in educational research and measurement and has held senior leadership positions at the state and national levels. As program manager for assessment at the Education Statistics Services Institute of the American Institutes for Research, she oversees about twenty projects, forty staff people, and budgets totaling about $6 million per year. Consultant, author, and presenter, Dr. Baldwin Anderson is an enthusiastic practitioner of Inspired Learning Facilitation. She has conducted national surveys of adults seeking alternative high school diplomas and has authored numerous papers and reports on the literacy skills, test performance, and academic achievement of adult learners. She received her BA degree with honors in English Literature from the University of Florida where she also undertook graduate study in childhood education, receiving the M.Ed. She earned the Ph.D. degree in measurement, statistics, and evaluation from the University of Maryland at College Park. Areas of special interest include measurement and evaluation of educational achievement, adult and experiential learning, coaching in organizations, and the development of professional and personal competence. Contact: jbanderson@earthlink.net.

Katherine Johnson, Ed.D., is a Certified Life Coach through Coach for Life. She is an international consultant, university professor, and coordinator of leadership programs. For over twenty years Dr. Johnson coordinated professional and organizational development opportunities for the nationally recognized Howard County Public School System. Currently she coordinates leadership coaches for high-level educational leaders. Dr. Johnson co-created the Coaching Skills for Educational Leaders program, a yearlong program that taught coaching skills to administrators and leaders in the school system. In addition, she teaches educational leadership and coaching courses for Johns Hopkins University and Loyola College, and leads Transformations-International, which focuses on coaching and consulting for individuals and organizations. She earned a Masters Degree from George Washington University and a Doctorate in Human Resource Development in Education from University of Maryland. Contact: DrKEJohnson@comcast.net

 *Peter Reding, MCC, is an international educator, coach, and visionary. He co-founded Coach for Life in 1996 as a spiritually-based coach training school. In 2003, he founded the Foundation for Inspired Learning to certify trainers and educators from all walks of life in the Inspired Learning Model. For 25 years Mr. Reding worked and taught in multinational corporations. He has conducted trainings from Australia, China, and Japan to the UK, Greece, and Portugal. Peter earned a BS degree in business from Marquette University and an MBA from Pepperdine University. He earned the International Coach Federation's Master Certified Coach credential. Mr. Reding's life's work is to transform the learning process, in the entire world, from a critical-based learning theory to one that acknowledges and celebrates every step towards the mastery of the learner's curiosities and passions. Contact: preding@inspiredlearning.org.*

Peer Coaching:
Enabling Skills Development and Diversity
Awareness in Corporate South Africa

Roger Maitland

The changing business and socio-political climate in South Africa, together with a global context marked by ecological degradation and globalisation, has meant that there is an increased need for lifelong learning. This research explores how peer relationships utilise coaching skills and processes to enhance professional development in the context of these needs.

This qualitative study with a narrative design focussed on world construction. Snowballing techniques were applied to find a sample of six relationship-pairs within Johannesburg Stock Exchange listed companies in South Africa. The sample was diverse in terms of gender and cultural groups. The data was analysed using an approach based on grounded theory.

This research found that peer-coaching offered unique advantages in supporting professional and personal development. Successful peer relationships were found to have three levels of mutuality; the exchange of knowledge, roles and rank. This supported empowerment in the relationship and enabled effective experiential learning.

Various coaching skills and processes were found to be operating in successful peers. Common values and clear purpose were established to be important in matching peers. For the relationship to sustain, the pace of development between the pair needed to be aligned. The development of professional and personal competencies was interlinked.

The study suggests that coaching as a discipline legitimises and develops peer coaching to increase the extent of its impact. Recommendations for the design of peer-based coaching interventions for organisations are given. It is also proposed that peer coaching be utilised to address diversity awareness and skills development.

Coaching is increasingly used for ongoing professional development within organisations both globally and in South Africa. The challenges, which organizations face as a result of globalisation and environmental degradation, as well as the transforming socio-political context and skills backlog in South Africa, have meant that additional vehicles for coaching delivery need to be considered by organisations.

Professional coaching is costly to roll out on a large scale and typically has been supplemented by mentoring or "manager as coach" programmes. Peer coaching has been found in this research to offer a preferred mode of delivery supporting diversity awareness, ongoing learning and professional development. This is particularly suited to the current trends in South African organisations, which rely on collaboration and interdependence in the marketplace.

Interdependence can be seen as a golden thread running through many current South African and global challenges. These economic, socio-political and environmental challenges (Capra, 1982) are likely to only be successfully addressed through collaborative learning, thinking and acting (Ploughman, 2000). This interdependence has lead to increasingly complex decision making in both the South African and global business environments, which can be seen to substantially accelerate the need for ongoing professional development and mutual support between employees.

This complexity, increased competition and job uncertainty has forced businesses and employees to take more risks (Ploughman, 2000). Ecological uncertainty further demands humankind to adapt and change (Capra, 1982). This current business climate of continuous change and uncertainty increased levels of anxiety that are associated with the stress of risk taking. This places further emphasis on the large scale of the need for continuous professional development.

The changing nature of organisational hierarchies further impacts the demands organisations make on their employees. Traditional notions of hierarchy are giving way to networks (Ploughman, 2000). Flatter organisational structures have resulted in employees having increased isolation and pressure due to managers' larger spans of control (Holbeche, 1996). Employees therefore need to learn how to operate effectively in increasingly projectised environments harnessing lateral resources.

South Africa has particular needs for professional and skills development in organisations deriving from the need to redress historic inequalities within education and labour (Suzman, 1994). Black economic empowerment and employment equity policies have accentuated the need for accelerated professional development. The fast changing national environment demands the co-creation of new solutions. This is often difficult from an expert or authority driven vehicle for professional development such as mentoring or "manager as coach" initiatives, where historic solutions are often imposed which limit new explorative thinking and collaboration.

Thus in both a global and South African context, organisations need to find innovative and effective ways to enhance professional development on an increasingly large scale. Peer coaching is submitted to be an invaluable vehicle to meet some of the above-mentioned needs.

Method

This exploratory study investigated how peer relationships utilise coaching skills and processes to enhance professional development within South African corporations. A qualitative approach was used with a narrative design focussing on world construction. The emphasis is on detailed description and understanding of phenomena within the appropriate context (Breakwell, Hammond, and Fife-Schaw, 1995).

Snowballing techniques were applied to find a sample of six relationship-pairs within Johannesburg Stock Exchange listed companies in South Africa. The sample was diverse in terms of gender and cultural groups. The data was analysed using an approach based on grounded theory.

Two interviews per participant were scheduled. In the initial 60-minute individual interview I attempted to establish rapport with the participant. To ensure consistency, a standardised statement of context and question was used to begin each interview. Subsequent to this, the interview was guided by a set of research questions. These were applied with some flexibility.

A second round of interviews was conducted after the individual interviews. These were 60-minute depth interviews, which sought to unpack themes that emerged from the initial round of interviews. Participants were also asked to complete reflection forms between the interviews that acted to focus their attention on the relationship between the two interviews, allowing for a deepening of their reflection in the second interview.

Transcriptions were reviewed for themes and hypotheses throughout. The associated process of data analysis was informed by Post and Andrews (1982), and involved exploring the data for categories, derived from preliminary hypotheses, which showed commonalities across cases.

Findings

This research found that peer relationships and consequently peer coaching offer unique advantages in supporting professional and personal development. Key findings are presented below.

Peer Relationships

Peer coaching needs to exist within a peer relationship. A peer relationship can be considered any relationship in which each party has a perception and experience of equality in the relationship (Kram and Isabella, 1985). One respondent expressed this as follows, "We both see each other on the same level."

Peer relations are quite distinct from traditional mentoring relationships in which the higher rank of one is continuously in focus, which creates a boundary in the relationships, limiting the dialogues to work-based topics. These relationships resulted in one of each pair not getting their needs adequately met. This often seemed to put the relationship at risk of termination. As one respondent commented, "I am beginning to wonder if the investment of my time was worthwhile."

Successful peer relationships were found to have three levels of mutuality, namely, the exchange of knowledge, roles, and rank. This supported empowerment in the relationship and enabled effective experiential learning. The following principles derived from the study are put forward as tenets of peer coaching:

- The exchange of information or knowledge was foundational to these relationships and was typically psychosocial and career enhancing. This demonstrated that there was an integration of personal and professional development in successful peer relationships. An important consideration for people engaging in peer coaching is that this exchange of information was most effective for learning when it was a real- time reflection.
- The exchange of roles allowed for a deepening of learning in the relationships.

- In successful examples of peer relationships, each partner in the pair would only temporarily take up the role of facilitator or coach. This is aligned with the principle of lifelong learning where continuous adaptation is required and the learning is never complete.

- Individuals participating in peer coaching should be aware that learning can take place both when coaching someone through an experiential learning cycle (Kolb, 1984) as well as when being coached. One participant described this phenomenon as follows, "I often bounce ideas off her, or phone her and share my thoughts, or blow off steam. So I draw on her as much as she draws on me."

- The exchange of rank was found to be present in effective peer relationships. Rank is used broadly to describe amongst others, holding authority, maturity, an expert role or a higher psychosocial awareness. The important factor is that both partners in the peer relationships had rank at different times in the relationship and that this rank was temporary, shifting from person to person.

- Adult learning is self-directed (Knowles, 1990); learners who feel empowered are more likely to take responsibility for their own learning. Acknowledgement of temporary rank can be considered important in peer coaching as it allows for one of the peers to lead the dialogue without taking power from the other peer.

Coaching Processes and Skills

The research shows that several criteria are essential if a peer relationship is to successfully act as a coaching relationship. Individuals engaging in peer coaching relationships should consider the following:

- Good matching is fundamental to a successful peer relationship. Peer coaches should work to find peers with common personal values. This enables the pair to use a common language towards life and work.

- In cases where the relationship pair was from different cultural backgrounds, differences around diversity still gave way to personal values. The point of connection in the relationship was seldom attributed to commonalities around cultures or cultural values,

  > I didn't know that Eddy[1] was coloured, when I met him…I always thought he was Greek…and then I wondered what his background was, because he was always just ahead of most of us in his way of thinking and talking.

- For a peer relationship to sustain, the rate of development of both partners in the pair needs to be similar. The misalignment of this factor resulted in judgments that prevented the pairs from seeing deeper problem contexts.

- Peer coaching relationships should attempt to adopt a stance of unconditional acceptance that enables vulnerability, curiosity, and learning.

- Peer relationships needed a clear and specific purpose. This is similar to formal coaching relationships (Flaherty, 1999; Peltier, 2001; Whitworth, Kimsey-House, and Sandahl, 1998). Peer coaching relationships should consider either a mutually understood and agreed purpose or link the relationship to external outcomes derived from an educational programme, project or work outcome.

Professional Development

In the peer relationships, there was little distinction between personal and professional development. Rather personal limitations and sensitivities were dealt with in the context of understanding that they had bearing on professional growth. When personal and professional developmental needs were both dealt with simultaneously, this seemed to lead to enhanced growth and performance, enabling the person to reinvent him or herself.

A broad range of professionally enhancing skills and development areas were covered in the relationships. Personal developmental skills are included in the peer-coaching category as this was handled simultaneously with professional development in these relationships. These are presented in Table 1 and contrasted to those of the relationships demonstrating more of a mentoring approach:

Peer Coaching	Mentoring Relationships
- Leadership skills - Broad range of psycho-social skills - Academic development - Diversity awareness - Decision making skills - Assertiveness skills - Systemic thinking (pragmatic)	- Technical skills - Skills transfer - Decision making skills - Self awareness skills

TABLE 1: Comparative relational outputs

Professional development could be seen in the peer relationships as a continuous process of adapting to the changing needs of the work environment. This can be viewed as a process of lifelong learning. This not only allows the individual to adapt to the work environment but also supports the individual participating in the ongoing process of adapting the work environment and organisational culture for more effective functioning. As one respondent noted, "Our departments have worked better together than ever before."

Diversity and Systemic Thinking

In this particular case, acceptance between a culturally diverse pair proved to be both a characteristic of the relationship as well as a learning outcome of it. When asked about the learning experienced through the relationship, the participant responded, "I think it was also tolerance to understand people... understand the person for what they are or who they are." The other participant in the relationship pair expressed an aligned view that she had learnt a "deep appreciation and tolerance" in her interpersonal relationships.

This deep appreciation for difference or diversity impacted on this participant's ability to think systemically. Whilst systemic theory was covered in a corporate university course that both participants attended, the relationship seemed to enable them to apply systems thinking pragmatically in the workplace. This Moslem participant, a financial manager, shared her deep appreciation for the Zulu participant, an IT manager in the same company, who was in the relationship pair with her. Their joint exploration of cultural differences was vast, in that they had worked, studied and travelled together. Furthermore, their families had become friends.

Through the relationship, the participant who is a financial manger reported to have developed an increased level of tolerance for individuals in the IT department. She linked this to her ability to understand the unique dynamics of the IT environment. These had often led to her and her colleagues in the financial department making unjustified assumptions about individuals in the IT department, particularly when there were IT problems in the department: "We sit on opposite sides and never blow up. We have a deep abiding respect and seem to know what the other one is thinking."

As a leader in the organisation she had passed this attitude on to her subordinates and actively encouraged a different approach based on tolerance and understanding in communications between the departments. As such, the joint functioning of the two departments had improved: "Our departments have worked better together than ever before."

As she reflected in the interview, she linked this experience to the improvement of her relationship with her manager who had shown an increased interest in understanding her cultural background. This increased their overall ability to communicate.

Recommendations

The findings of this study affirm the success of what could be termed peer coaching, and put forward that peer relationships successfully utilise coaching skills to enhance professional and personal development. The practical application of the findings will now be considered.

Organisational Interventions

The findings of this study suggest several implications for organisations. General recommendations are given for designing organisational interventions based on peer relationships. Peer coaching has been found to be particularly suited to the development of leaders and accelerated development processes on the basis of their pragmatic emphasis and reflective component.

Peer coaching can also effectively support succession planning in bridging the gap between manager and owner or business executive. The mutual exchange of knowledge, rank and roles, as demonstrated in the study, would support a gradual process towards the equality of perceived rank between the two.

It is proposed that peer-coaching interventions should be designed around a particular area of focus within personal or professional development such as leadership development or an accelerated development programme. The findings suggest that peer relationships are most effective when used in tandem with a structured learning programme with clear objectives.

Peers should be matched in pairs in a way that ensures an alignment of personal values and should include consideration of levels of ambition. In the findings, ambition was linked to pace of development and was shown to be an important indicator of the sustainability of the relationship. Furthermore, peers should experience a personal fit and a sense of equality between them.

The positioning of peers in a relationship-pair was found to be of significance in this study, as it facilitates the peer thinking systemically in viewing other parts of the organisational system. Pairing individuals across different divisions, national offices or organisations is likely to increase learning outputs and value-adds.

The intervention design should prescribe a structure for meetings, reviews and objectives. Peers should practice mutual exchange of information along with the exchange of roles and rank.

A further recommendation is that review sessions, which could take the form of action learning sets, or group dialogue or individual professional coaching sessions, be periodically arranged to facilitate a reflection on learning and/or the relationship. In the study, the process of interviewing was shown in several cases to deepen the participant's learning from their relationship.

Developing Diversity Awareness

The results suggest that peer relationships offer a unique contribution to developing diversity awareness within organisations. Peer relationships were found to effectively enhance the ability of each peer to respect and understand difference, as well as develop effective interpersonal skills. This enabled them to work across sociocultural barriers and influenced peers' ability to think systemically. This meant that they were better able to consider the relative perspectives emerging from different positions in various parts of the organisational system.

In a South African context, post-apartheid sensitivities toward authority seemed to act as a barrier to communication in mentoring relationships with positional power. Currently in South Africa, the workplace is likely to be one of the only forums in which diverse cultural groups, on a large scale, are forced to inter-relate in a meaningful way. It is therefore a useful point of leverage for the development of diversity awareness that underpins the social reconstruction of the South African population.

The study indicated that not only were peers more able to adapt to their environment, they also played a part in shaping the evolution of organisational cultural norms. It can be argued that this is a crucial aspect of social reconstruction, which enables the formation of a new social culture operating across the diverse historical sociocultural groupings.

Peer coaching goes beyond the common use of "manager as coach" in emphasising equality rather than rank or positional power in the relationship. This enhances the ability of peer coaching relationships to raise and work with diversity in culture, gender and other areas.

Implications for Coaching

The research affirms the need for coaching as a discipline to consider the use of peer relationships in the workplace as a legitimate platform within which coaching processes and skills can be effectively utilised. Moving beyond direct commercial relationships offers a potential point of leverage for the discipline to make a substantial contribution to the development of society at large.

This research is not claiming that the use of peer coaching replaces the need for a professional coach. Rather, I am claiming that peer relationships offer an effective platform for coaching to be practised, and that this platform offers several unique advantages that can be harnessed.

The professional coach can thus engage in direct relationships, as well as training and facilitating peer based coaching interventions. Internal coaching can be particularly effective in a South African organisational context by responding to rank sensitivities and working within relationships based on equality rather than relationships influenced strongly by positional power.

It would seem that there is an opportunity for coaching as a discipline to move beyond current concerns about service delivery to effectively address local and global challenges pertaining to globalisation, diversity, ecology and power.

Concluclusion

Peer coaching has been shown to be a viable and effective delivery vehicle to enhance personal and professional development on a sustainable basis. Several advantages have been identified whereby peer coaching has been shown to be particularly suited to supporting South African organisations develop diversity awareness and accelerate the skills development process within the workplace.

References

Breakwell, G. M., Hammond, S., & Fife-Schaw, C. (Eds.). (1995). *Research methods in psychology.* London: Sage.

Capra, F. (1982). *The turning point: Science, society and the rising culture.* New York, NY: Simon & Schuster.

Flaherty, J. (1999) *Coaching: Evoking excellence in others.* Boston, MA: Butterworth Heinemann.

Holbeche, L. (1996). Peer mentoring: The challenges and opportunities. *Career Development International, 1*(7): 24-27.

Knowles, M. (1994). *The adult learner: A neglected species* (3rd Ed.). Houston, TX: Gulf Publishing Company.

Kolb, D. (1984). *Experiential learning: Experience as the source of learning and development.* Englewood Cliffs, NJ: Prentice-Hall.

Kram, K. E., & Isabella, L. (1985). Mentoring alternatives: The role of peer relationships in career development. *Academy of Management Journal, 28,* 110-132.

Peltier, B. (2001). *The psychology of executive coaching: Theory and application.* New York, NY: Brunner-Routledge.

Plougman, L. (2000). *Transformational leadership.* Stellenbosch: University of Stellenbosch Press.

Post, J. E., & Andrews, P. N. (1982). Case research in corporate and society studies. In L. Preston (Ed.). *Research in Corporate Social Performance and Policy, 4,* 1-33. Greenwich, CT: JAI Press.

Suzman, H. (1994). *In no uncertain terms.* London: Mandarin.

Whitworth, L., Kimsey-House, H., & Sandahl, P. (1998). *Co-active coaching: New skills for coaching people towards success in work and life.* Palo Alto, CA: Davies Black Publishing.

[1] Names of interviewees have been changed to ensure confidentiality.

Roger Maitland is a corporate coach and director of LifeLab. His coaching focuses on leadership development, career transitions, and the link between personal identity and career path. He provides process facilitation, peer coaching interventions, and HIV/AIDS care and support programs. Mr. Maitland developed the coach training program of the South African College of Applied Psychology (SACAP) and is a member of the quality assurance committee of SACAP as well as the research committee of the Coaching and Mentoring Council of South Africa (COMENSA). He earned a Masters Degree in coaching from Middlesex University (UK) and an Honours Degrees in psychology. Contact: roger@lifelab.biz

Inviting a Dialogue About Core Coaching Competencies

Jeffrey E. Auerbach

The process of International Coach Federation (ICF) coach credentialing and accreditation of coach training programs revolves around the individual coach, or the coach training organization, demonstrating sufficient muster in the eleven ICF core competencies.

The "Portfolio Committee" developed the eleven ICF core competencies in 1999. This study evaluates how the existing eleven core competencies were identified and reports on a pilot survey of forty coaching competencies rated by twenty-nine coaches. This paper examines whether coaches currently view the eleven ICF coaching competencies as the most important competencies to be an effective coach. In addition, preliminary findings are briefly reported of a survey in which 565 coaches rated which competencies, or skills, are most important to valuable coaching.

Nine of the eleven ICF core coaching competencies are identified as highly important by the coaches in the survey and three additional competencies that are not named by ICF are identified. The three competencies that were identified in this survey that are not specifically listed as ICF competencies are "lifelong training and development," "managing obstacles," and "thought partner."

The top twelve coaching competencies identified by the participants, in no particular order, were: lifelong training and development; establishing trust and intimacy with the client; coaching presence; powerful questioning; designing actions; managing progress and accountability; direct communication; active listening; creating awareness; thought partner; planning and goal setting; and managing obstacles.

The competency survey indicates that the ICF core coaching competencies developed six years ago are still considered important to coaches although other competencies are also deemed uniquely valuable to be an outstanding coach.

Different coaching competencies are necessary depending on the needs of the client - complicating the identification of a core set of coaching competencies. The author cautions that as research continues into coaching competencies the value of the coach's wisdom, creativity, and professional judgment should not be constrained by an over reliance on any specific set of coaching competency guidelines.

Introduction

As coaching has expanded, the number of coach training programs has also grown, from eight in 1999, to thirty International Coach Federation (ICF) Accredited Coach Training Programs in April 2005. In addition, an estimated 145 additional coach training programs exist, albeit not accredited by the International Coach Federation (Peer Resources, 2005).

Although there are many for-profit organizations certifying coaches, the largest non-profit coaching professional organization, with an elected board of directors, is the ICF. A goal of the ICF is to maintain the coaching industry as a self-governing industry. Most media covering coaching emphasizes the need for the client to work with a trained, certified coach noting that since coaching is not regulated any individual can claim to be a coach. The drive to certify or "accredit" coaches lead to the development of an accreditation process by the ICF. In 1999 the "grandfathering" period of ICF accreditation ended. Since then coaches have become credentialed through either completing a "portfolio application" or a "graduate of an accredited coach training program" application process. Central to this process are the eleven ICF core coaching competencies. The credentialing of individual coaches and the approval of an "Accredited Coach Training Program" both revolve around the coach that is applying for credentialing, or the school that is applying for accreditation, as demonstrating sufficient muster, or a curriculum rooted in the eleven ICF Professional Coaching Core Competencies.

There is growing interest from coaching practitioners, researchers and some coach training organizations for increased dialogue and research on evidence-based coaching, coaching effectiveness, and coaching competencies and their application to the coach training process (Stober, 2004, 2005; Grant, 2004).

Purpose of the Study

The fact that both individual coaches and coach training programs are approved based on a demonstration of these eleven ICF core coaching competencies begs the question of how these eleven core competencies were developed. Are these competencies most needed for effective coaching, in most situations, and are they the best competencies for coach training programs to make a centerpiece of their curriculum?

In this paper we will examine the selection of the eleven core competencies, review research related to coaching roles and how they relate to coaching competencies, and analyze whether or not coaches currently identify the eleven ICF core competencies as among the most important competencies to be an effective coach. In addition recommendations and cautions are indicated for future research.

How Were the Core Competencies Developed?

No information on how these eleven core coaching competencies came to be selected has been published previously in a scholarly journal. Through a series of electronic communications with several past and current ICF board members the following description of the process was obtained.

In 1998 a committee entitled the "Portfolio Committee" was formed and chaired by Pam Richarde and Laura Whitworth. The committee was made up of the founders or senior faculty of the eight best-known coaching schools of the time. The intent was to agree upon coaching competencies and then create a portfolio exam for use by ICF that reflected these competencies. The current listing of the eleven core competencies was published on the ICF website in March 1999.

In the selection process the committee members emphasized the knowledge, skills, abilities, and personal characteristics that they considered were reflected in a competent coach. At the end of the process all of the eight coaching schools' representatives affirmed that the ICF core coaching competencies were ones that each committee member could support 100%, and that the schools' model of coaching and training incorporated the ICF competencies at least as a minimum (Richarde, 2005; Reding, 2005).

The process of selecting the eleven competencies and specific selection of identified behaviors has been described by one of the committee members as "part majority and part intuitive." In addition, there was a desire to develop competencies that when taken as a whole would distinguish a competent coach from a competent therapist, consultant, teacher, manager, friend, or mentor.

The intent of the committee was that the competencies developed would apply to every type of professional coach. Further, the committee specified which competencies would be used in every coaching session and which competencies were important for a competent coach to be able to use, when appropriate, in particular situations (Reding, 2005).

This determination of the eleven core coaching competencies adopted by ICF is based on an "expert model" where a group of experts determined, based on their experience, which competencies are most important. What was not evaluated in a systematic manner was whether the client obtains better results by working with a coach who utilizes these eleven core competencies appropriately than by working with a coach who utilizes a somewhat different set of core coaching competencies. That research is beyond the scope of this paper but would be a valuable study.

Background on Competencies in Coaching

For the purposes of examining professional coaching, a competency is defined as the knowledge, skills, attitudes and behaviors that differentiate level of effectiveness. In one example of defining a competency, an individual who is seen as a "change catalyst" would need to demonstrate the following four behaviors with particular frequency:

1. Defines general need for change
2. Expresses vision for change
3. Acts to support change
4. Personally leads change (Boyatzis, Goleman and Hay/McBer, 1999)

Grant (2004) reported that since 1937 there were only 122 peer reviewed academic papers specifically focused on professional coaching. However, only one of those articles, "Executive Coaching: The Need for Standards of Competence" (Brotman, Liberi, and Wasylshyn, 1998), and only one coaching book (Auerbach, 2005), specifically addressed coaching "competence" in the title.

Especially relevant to examining the competencies of an effective coach is the "competency" approach designed to predict the outcome of effectiveness in various occupations, often with a primary emphasis on managers and leaders (McClelland, 1973;

Boyatzis, 1982; Lombardo and Eichenger, 1999). In this competency approach, specific capabilities are identified and validated against effectiveness measures, or often inductively discovered and then articulated as competencies. McClelland and Boyatzis's work suggests that it is insufficient to solely rely on the expert model of identifying the competencies of coaching, stopping there and then recommending that these competencies are what needs to be taught and what coaches need to be evaluated on. The next step is to analyze successful outcomes and then identify coaching competencies that have criterion-related validation. Perhaps one of the best methods to identify coaching competencies would include a combination of direct observation of coaching sessions over time, then an assessment of outcomes; an appreciative inquiry related survey of experienced coaches of successful coaching encounters; and an analysis of coaching outcomes using criterion sampling.

One of the most common methods of developing specific articulations of competencies is the critical incident technique (Flanagan, 1954) where the objective is to identify specific and concrete behaviors that designate a person as outstanding or inadequate in his or her role. This technique would require that observers who are aware of the aims and objectives of coaching observe effective coaches for a specific time period and log specific coaching behaviors, and skills, that are linked to effective or ineffective outcomes.

There are a large number of potential coaching competencies. A complete list of the types of knowledge and tools that comprise the competencies is beyond the scope of this paper. However, they would include a wide range of attitudes, skills, and techniques such as: relationship building, use of assessments, 360-degree feedback, insight, competency development, dialogue skills, systems-based approaches, listening skills, questioning skills, cultural awareness, diversity, psychological knowledge and business knowledge (Peterson, 1996; Tobias, 1996; Kiel, Rimmer, Williams, and Doyle, 1996; Katz and Miller, 1996; Levinson, 1996; Saporito, 1996; Witherspoon and White 1996; and Stein 1993a).

A complication in the development of coaching competencies is the variety of coaching being practiced in the marketplace. For example, Witherspoon and White (1996) report there are four different roles that coaches often play when coaching in organizations. In some cases, different competencies would be most important depending on the role of the coach: skills, performance, development, and the wide-open "thought partner" role of coaching a senior executive. Auerbach (2001) identified the four most common executive coaching roles, in order of frequency; 1) aiding in the development of effective executive skills, 2) identifying and modifying managerial style to improve the effectiveness of individuals and teams, 3) helping executives identify and utilize key strengths, and 4) aiding in the adaptation to change. These frequent roles suggest that competency in the technical areas of executive and leadership development and the recent research in positive psychology would be especially relevant, yet these knowledge domains are not mentioned in the eleven ICF core competency areas.

Research of the ICF membership (Grant and Zackon, 2004) found that 19% have prior employment in the mental health fields, whereas 31% have primarily management experience, representing substantially different college education and work experience. This diversity suggests a differing set of competencies, and development needs, of new coaches moving into coach training programs. Stein (2003b) points out that there are at least nine professional areas that coaching draws on that serve as roots for the coaching field. Numerous early leaders in the field of psychology, Jung, Frankel, Adler, and Maslow, as well as current contributors, such as Seligman (2002), Goleman, Boyatzis and McKee (2002), Kouzes and Posner (2002), and Csikszentmihalyi (2002) have espoused development approaches that have not been limited to the treatment of pathology, but also mirrored what coaches now engage in such as focusing on methods to more fully develop oneself, obtain a clearer vision of one's life in line with vision and values, and engage in action learning activities (Auerbach, 2001). Again this points to a myriad of potential competencies – specific skills, knowledge, techniques, and behaviors that could be linked to effective coaching outcomes. To further complicate the range of desired competencies in a coach, moreover, amongst ICF 2004 Conference attendees, 32% indicate their primary work area is personal coaching and 30% indicate their primary focus is on executive coaching – again suggesting that there may be different competencies linked to whether one's focus is personal coaching or executive coaching (International Coach Federation Conference Evaluation, Final Report, December 2004).

Demographics

The survey participants were 76% female and 24% male and all had completed a coach-training program or were enrolled in an ICF coach-training curriculum at the College of Executive Coaching. A pre-requisite for admission in this program is the possession of a graduate degree so 100% of the participants had either a Master's or Doctoral Degree in fields such as psychology, business administration, social work, education, or organizational development. The median length of time that the participants had been earning at least 25% of their income in coaching was 2.7 years with a range of less that one year to fifteen years.

Table 1: Demographic data of the 29 survey respondents.

Gender
• Male: 7
• Female: 22
Age
• Median: 48
• Range: 28-56
Years Coaching
• Median: 2.7
• Range: >1 - 15

Method and Evaluation of Competencies

A random sample of 90 coaches were sent via email a 40-item pilot coaching competency questionnaire and asked to select the 20 competencies that they believed were most important for them to be an outstanding coach. Twenty-nine valid surveys were returned and scored. The percentages indicating how frequently the participants identified a particular competency as one of the twenty most important competencies are reported in this paper.

The forty coaching competencies, included (a) a verbatim listing of the eleven ICF coaching competencies, (b) a verbatim listing of an additional twelve executive coaching core competencies (Brotman, Liberi and Wasylyshyn, 1998) which had been adapted from the Career Architect (1992), plus (c) additional competencies, including technical skills, competencies, and coaching approaches, such as "use of assessments," "values identification and clarification," and "thought partner" identified by the author from other senior personal and executive coaches.

Responses to the Coaching Competency Survey

Twenty-nine valid survey responses were received. Table 2 indicates the percentage of respondents that identified the respective competency as one of the twenty most important competencies to be an outstanding coach. The top twelve competencies identified by the participants, in no particular order, were:

- Lifelong Training and Development
- Establishing Trust and Intimacy with the Client
- Coaching Presence
- Powerful Questioning
- Designing Actions
- Managing Progress and Accountability
- Direct Communication
- Active Listening
- Creating Awareness
- Thought Partner
- Planning and Goal Setting
- Managing Obstacles

Of the eleven ICF core coaching competencies nine are in the top twelve identified in this study. The only two ICF coaching competencies that were not identified in the top twelve were "Meeting ethical guidelines and professional standards" and "establishing the coaching agreement." The three competencies that were identified in this survey as in the top twelve that are not specifically listed in the ICF competencies are "lifelong training and development," "managing obstacles," and "thought partner. (See Table 2).

Table 2
Percentage of Respondents Indicating: One of Twenty Most Important Competencies Needed To Be An Outstanding Coach.
(Abbreviated description of Competency Survey – See Appendix for Full Survey Behavioral Descriptors.)

Number	Competency Description	Percentage
1.	Lifelong Training and Development	62%
2.	Empathetic Listening	41%
3.	Body Language and Communication Style	17%
4.	Establishing Trust and Intimacy with the Client	79%
5.	Approachability	48%
6.	Comfort Around Top Management	7%
7.	Compassion	38%
8.	Creativity	45%
9.	Customer Focus	17%
10.	Meeting Ethical Guidelines and Professional Standards	55%
11.	Establishing the Coaching Agreement	59%
12.	Acceptance and Respect	41%
13.	Coaching Presence	79%
14.	Utilization of Coaching Tools	28%
15.	Powerful Questioning	83%
16.	Goal Formation and Clarification	48%
17.	Empowerment	52%
18.	Designing Actions	69%
19.	Establishing and Maintaining Accountability	24%
20.	Managing Progress and Accountability	66%
21.	Integrity and Trust	59%
22.	Intellectual Horsepower	10%
23.	Interpersonal Savvy	45%
24.	Direct Communication	66%
25.	Dealing With Paradox	21%
26.	Political Savvy	17%
27.	Self-Knowledge	59%
28.	Active Listening	76%
29.	Values Identification and Clarification	38%
30.	Challenges to Break Out	38%
31.	Resource Identification	31%
32.	Use of Assessments	41%
33.	Creating Awareness	66%
34.	Imagining the Successful Outcome	31%
35.	Managing Obstacles	62%
36.	Identifying Mental Models	17%
37.	Thought Partner	66%
38.	Planning and Goal Setting	62%
39.	Encouraging the Client's Dreams	24%
40.	Commitment to Outcomes	34%

Discussion of Findings

This paper seemingly makes the assumption that identifying the competencies of an effective coach is a useful undertaking. Not all authors agree with this premise. Ferrar (2004, p. 53) quotes the European Mentoring and Coaching Council (EMCC) as having commissioned a project to "...establish whether there is an underlying set of core competencies common to all types of coaching and mentoring practice " and to "...identify whether it is possible to draw existing standards and competencies for all types of coaching and mentoring into a common framework."

Ferrar (2004) observes the cautiousness of the EMCC in examining the concept of competencies in coaching, and argues that there are limits to the usefulness of competencies and points out that the complexities of context can make an overemphasis on setting standards and evaluating competence, at the expense of exercising contextual based professional judgment. As an example, he points to the well-developed UK based system of the National Vocational Qualifications as having had little positive impact on the customer's experience in the financial services industry.

Moreover, it's important to remember that this study was not designed to illustrate a complete list of coaching competencies. Nor does this study attempt to specify which is the most important coaching competency. Rather it identifies that a group of competencies are deemed to be fundamental to be an outstanding coach in these research participants' opinion, and that there are other competencies that also are deemed important that are not addressed explicitly in the ICF competencies. Furthermore it is observed that the ICF core competencies did make up the majority of the competencies that these coaches identified as most important.

A difficulty in evaluating existing lists of coaching competencies is that different authors have described the competencies with varying degrees of depth and clarity. For example, "coaching presence" as described by ICF includes a conglomeration of behaviors, and is 112 words in length; "designing actions" is 184 words in length; and "powerful questioning" has 84 words. Whereas, Brotman et al. (1998), use 41 words to describe "dealing with paradox." The impact of the longer competency descriptions is the respondent may conclude the longer description is more in-depth, hence more important. A useful next step would be for the language of the existing ICF core coaching competencies to be refined and shortened while maintaining the central meaning of the competencies.

A range of explanations is available for why the ICF core coaching competencies are overall deemed as the most important. For example, these core competencies are emphasized in coach training programs, which have the effect of convincing coaches that they must be the most important competencies. Also, two of the three other, non-ICF competencies that made the top twelve in this study, "managing obstacles" and "thought partner," happen to be competencies that are strongly emphasized in the coach training program that the sample was drawn from. Of course, the results may also be a reflection that the ICF competencies were the longest and most detailed of the competencies listed in the survey, and the results may also indicate that the ICF committee did an outstanding job in identifying and describing key coaching competencies.

Considering the breadth of the public that is served by coaches and the specialization of some coaches it is evident that some competencies may be more important in some client situations, and at some times, than others. Although there may be some competencies that may be more important in executive coaching than in personal coaching, in general there appear to be many competencies that are fundamental to all professional coaching. Moreover, there may be some competencies that are so fundamental – even if they are not always so simple to execute – that many coaches don't consider them "coaching" competencies. Hence, the top twelve competencies identified by the competency survey did not include "meeting ethical guidelines and professional standards" and "establishing the coaching agreement". Several coaches contacted about these competencies commented that these two were so basic and central to conducting a professional interaction that they did not consider them as a central competency unique to coaching – it was as if they saw these as "standard operating procedure" in any professional relationship.

This pilot study utilized a relatively small sample size. Increasing the number of survey responses would increase the effectiveness of the study. A subsequent study was conducted. The 2005 State of the Coaching Industry Research Project (Auerbach, 2005), with a different emphasis, but one of the questions posed is relevant to this article. The open-ended question was posed, "what competencies, skills or personal characteristics do you believe are most important to be a valued coach?" Respondents entered their own responses. The top three responses were: (a) listening, (b) integrity, and (c) effective questioning.

Conclusion

The competency survey indicates that the ICF core coaching competencies developed six years ago are still considered centrally important to coaches although other competencies are also deemed uniquely valuable to be an outstanding coach.

Although there may be different opinions on which competencies are most essential and future research studies may continue to delineate important competencies and specific behavioral descriptors, the value and intention of delineating what works, and what does not, is important to provide the best value for our clients and strengthen the coaching field. However, the value of the coach's wisdom, creativity, and professional judgment should not be constrained by an over-reliance on any specific set of coaching competency guidelines.

References

Auerbach, J. (2001). *Personal and executive coaching: The complete guide for mental health professionals.* Pismo Beach, CA: Executive College Press.

Auerbach, J. (2005). *Building competence in personal and executive coaching.* Pismo Beach, CA: College of Executive Coaching.

Boyatzis, R.E. (1982). *The competent manager: A model for effective performance.* New York, NY: Wiley & Sons.

Boyatzis, R., Goleman, D., & Hay/McBer. (1999) *Emotional competence inventory.* Boston, MA: Hay Group.

Brotman, L., Liberi, W., Wasylyshyn, K. (1998). Executive coaching: The need for standards of competence. *Consulting Psychology Journal. 50*(1), 40-46.

Career Architect (Version 2.2B) [Computer software]. (1992). Minneapolis, MN: Lominger Limited.

Csikszentmihalyi, M. (2002). *Good business: Leadership, flow, and the making of meaning.* New York: Penguin.

Ferrar, P. (2004). Reflections from the field. 53-60. *International Journal of Evidence Based Coaching and Mentoring. 2*(2) p. 53.

Flanagan, J. C. (1954). The critical incident technique. *Psychological Bulletin, 51,* 327-358.

Goleman, D., Boyatzis, R., & McKee, A. (2002). *Primal leadership.* NewYork, NY: Bantam Books.

Grant, A. (2004). Keeping up with the cheese! Research as a foundation for professional coaching of the future. In I. F. Stein & L. Belsten (Eds.), *Proceedings of the First ICF Coaching Research Symposium* (pp. 1-19). Mooresville, NC: Paw Print.

Grant, A. & Zackon, R. (2004). Executive, workplace and life coaching: Findings from a large-scale survey of international coach federation members. *International Journal of Evidence Based Coaching and Mentoring. 2*(2) 1-15.

International Coach Federation. (2004). *ICF Conference Evaluation, Final Report, December 2004.* AWP Research.

Katz, J. H. & Miller, F. (1996). Coaching leaders through culture change. *Consulting Psychology Journal: Practice and Research, 48,* 104-114.

Kiel, F., Rimmer, E., Williams, K., & Doyle, M. (1996). Coaching at the top. *Consulting Psychology Journal: Practice and Research, 48,* 67-77.

Kouzes, J. & Posner, B. (2002). *The Leadership challenge.* San Francisco, CA: Wiley & Sons.

Levinson, H. (1996). Executive coaching. *Consulting Psychology Journal: Practice and Research, 48,* 115-123.

Lombardo, M. & Eichenger, R. (1999). *Validity of the Leadership Architect Competencies.* http://www.lominger.com, Retrieved on April 28, 2005.

McClelland, D.C. (1973). Testing for competence rather than for "intelligence." *American Psychologist.* (1) 1-14.

Peterson, D.B. (1996). Executive coaching at work: The art of one-on-one change. *Consulting Psychology Journal: Practice and Research, 48,* 78-86.

Peer Resources (2005) *Coach training programs.* http://www.peer.ca/coaching.html. Retrieved on April 28, 2005.

Reding, P. (2005). Electronic communication on April 11, 2005.

Richarde, P. (2005). Electronic communication on April 18, 2005.

Seligman, M. (2002). *Authentic happiness: Using the new positive psychology to realize your potential for lasting fulfillment.* New York, NY: Simon & Schuster.

Saporito, T. J. (1996). Business-linked executive development: Coaching senior executives. *Consulting Psychology Journal: Practice and Research, 48,* 96-103.

Stein, I. F. (2004a) The coach-approach as dialogic discourse. In I. F. Stein, & L. Belsten (Eds.), *Proceedings of the First ICF Coaching Research Symposium* (pp. 130-139). Mooresville, NC: Paw Print Press.

Stein, I. F. (2004b) Beginning a promising conversation. In I. F. Stein, & L. Belsten (Eds.), *Proceedings of the First ICF Coaching Research Symposium* (pp. viii-xii). Mooresville, NC: Paw Print Press.

Stober, D. R. (2005). Coaching eye for the research guy and research eye for coaching guy: 20/20 vision for coaching through the scientist-practitioner model. In I. F. Stein, F. Campone, & L. J. Page (Eds.), *Proceedings Of the Second ICF Coaching Research Symposium,* (pp. 1 – 19). Washington, DC: International Coach Federation.

Tobias, L. L. (1996). Coaching executives. *Consulting Psychology Journal: Practice and Research, 48,* 87-95.

Witherspoon, R. & White, R. P. (1996). Executive coaching: A continuum of roles. *Consulting Psychology Journal: Practice and Research, 48,* 124-133.

Appendix

Percentage of Respondents Indicating: "One of Twenty Most Important Competencies Needed To Be An Outstanding Coach" (Verbatim listing of competencies)

- **Acceptance and Respect:** Coach creates an environment of acceptance and respect for the client to work in. (41%)
- **Active Listening:** Ability to focus completely on what the client is saying and is not saying, to understand the meaning of what is said in the context of the client's desires, and to support client self-expression; attends to the client and the client's agenda, and not to the coach's agenda for the client; hears the client's concerns, goals, values and beliefs about what is and is not possible; distinguishes between the words, the tone of voice, and the body language; summarizes, paraphrases, reiterates, mirrors back what client has said to ensure clarity and understanding; encourages, accepts, explores and reinforces the client's expression of feelings, perceptions, concerns, beliefs, suggestions, etc.; integrates and builds on client's ideas and suggestions; "bottom-lines" or understands the essence of the client's communication and helps the client get there rather than engaging in long descriptive stories; allows the client to vent or "clear" the situation without judgment or attachment in order to move on to next steps. (76%)
- **Approachability:** Is easy to approach and talk to; spends the extra effort to put others at ease; can be warm, pleasant, and gracious; is sensitive to and patient with interpersonal anxieties of others; builds rapport well; is a good listener. (48%)
- **Body Language and Communication Style:** Coach identifies and responds congruently within the client's body language, communication style and

representational system (visual, auditory, kinesthetic, modalities.) (17%)

- **Challenges to Break Out:** Creatively use questions to help the client consider if there are new, better ways to proceed…breaking out and moving beyond the status quo. (38%)

- **Coaching Presence:** Ability to be fully conscious and create spontaneous relationship with the client, employing a style that is open, flexible and confident; is present and flexible during the coaching process, dancing in the moment; accesses own intuition and trusts one's inner knowing - "goes with the gut"; is open to not knowing and takes risks; sees many ways to work with the client, and chooses in the moment what is most effective; uses humor effectively to create lightness and energy; confidently shifts perspectives and experiments with new possibilities for own action; demonstrates confidence in working with strong emotions, and can self-manage and not be overpowered or enmeshed by client's emotions. (79%)

- **Comfort Around Top Management:** Can deal comfortably with senior executives; understands how top executives think and process information; can talk their language and respond to their needs; can craft approaches likely to be seen as appropriate, efficient, and positive. (7%)

- **Commitment to Outcomes:** Maintain a focus on client-desired outcomes. (34%)

- **Compassion:** Genuinely cares about people; is concerned about their work and non-work problems; is available and ready to help; demonstrates real empathy with the joys, frustrations, and pain of others. (38%)

- **Creating Awareness:** Ability to integrate and accurately evaluate multiple sources of information, and to make interpretations that help the client to gain awareness and thereby achieve agreed-upon results; goes beyond what is said in assessing client's concerns, not getting hooked by the client's description; invokes inquiry for greater understanding, awareness and clarity; identifies for the client his/her underlying concerns, typical and fixed ways of perceiving himself/herself and the world, differences between the facts and the interpretation, disparities between thoughts, feelings and action; helps clients to discover for themselves the new thoughts, beliefs, perceptions, emotions, moods, etc. that strengthen their ability to take action and achieve what is important to them; communicates broader perspectives to clients and inspires commitment to shift their viewpoints and find new possibilities for action; helps clients to see the different, interrelated factors that affect them and their behaviors (e.g., thoughts, emotions, body, background); expresses insights to clients in ways that are useful and meaningful for the client; identifies major strengths vs. major areas for learning and growth, and what is most important to address during coaching; asks the client to distinguish between trivial and significant issues, situational vs. recurring behaviors, when detecting a separation between what is being stated and what is being done. (66%)

- **Creativity:** Can formulate new and unique ideas, easily makes connections among previously unrelated notions in ways that yield novel problem solving and/or plans for the future. (45%)

- **Customer Focus:** Is dedicated to meeting the expectations and requirements of internal and external customers, establishes and maintains effective relationships with customers and gains their trust and respect. (17%)

- **Dealing With Paradox:** Is very flexible and adaptable; can act in ways that seem contradictory; can be both tough and compassionate, empathic and objective; can be self-confident and appropriately humble; is seen as balanced despite the conflicting demands of a situation. (21%)

- **Designing Actions:** Ability to create with the client opportunities for ongoing learning, during coaching and in work/life situations, and for taking new actions that will most effectively lead to agreed-upon coaching results; brainstorms and assists the client to define actions that will enable the client to demonstrate, practice and deepen new learning; helps the client to focus on and systematically explore specific concerns and opportunities that are central to agreed-upon coaching goals; engages the client to explore alternative ideas and solutions, to evaluate options, and to make related decisions; promotes active experimentation and self-discovery, where the client applies what has been discussed and learned during sessions immediately afterwards in his/her work or life setting; celebrates client successes and capabilities for future growth; challenges client's assumptions and perspectives to provoke new ideas and find new possibilities for action; advocates or brings forward points of view that are aligned with client goals and, without attachment, engages the client to consider them; helps the client "do it now" during the coaching session, providing immediate support; encourages stretches and challenges but also a comfortable pace of learning. (69%)

- **Direct Communication:** Ability to communicate effectively during coaching sessions, and to use language that has the greatest positive impact on the client; is clear, articulate and direct in sharing and providing feedback; reframes and articulates to help the client understand from another perspective what he/she wants or is uncertain about; clearly states coaching objectives, meeting agenda, purpose of techniques or exercises; uses language appropriate and respectful to the client (e.g., non-sexist, non-racist, non-technical, non-jargon); uses metaphor and analogy to help to illustrate a point or paint a verbal picture. (66%)

- **Empathetic Listening:** Accurate reflection of the client's emotional state. (41%)

- **Empowerment:** Engage in behaviors that tend to lead a client to feel empowered versus dependent. (52%)

- **Encouraging the Client's Dreams:** Facilitate the client in identifying life-long meaningful dreams that enrich the client's life in a deeply satisfying manner. (24%)

- **Establishing and Maintaining Accountability:** Facilitate client following through on their selected action steps and goals in a manner that encourages self-reliance with minimal dependence. (24%)

- **Establishing the Coaching Agreement:** Ability to understand what is required in the specific coaching interaction and to come to agreement with the prospective and new client about the coaching process and relationship; understands and effectively discusses with the client the guidelines and specific parameters of the coaching relationship (e.g., logistics, fees, scheduling, inclusion of others if appropriate); reaches agreement about what is appropriate in the relationship and what is not, what is and is not being offered, and about the client's and coach's responsibilities; determines whether there is an effective match between his/her coaching method and the needs of the prospective client. (59%)

- **Establishing Trust and Intimacy with the Client:** Ability to create a safe, supportive environment that produces ongoing mutual respect and trust; shows genuine concern for the client's welfare and future; continuously demonstrates personal integrity, honesty and sincerity; establishes clear agreements and keeps promises; demonstrates respect for client's perceptions; learning style, personal being; provides ongoing support for and champions new behaviors and actions, including those involving risk taking and fear of failure; asks permission to coach client in sensitive, new areas. (79%)

- **Goal Formation and Clarification:** Client and Coach establish clear and inspiring positive goals congruent with Client's values. (48%)
  Identifying Mental Models: Identify assumptions and mental models, and help client select adaptive perspectives on challenges. (17%)

- **Imagining the Successful Outcome:** Facilitates the client seeing himself achieving the desired outcome. (31%)

- **Integrity and Trust:** Is widely trusted; is seen as a direct, truthful individual; can present the unvarnished truth in an appropriate and helpful manner; keeps confidences. (59%)

- **Intellectual Horsepower:** Is bright and intelligent; deals with concepts and complexity comfortably; described as intellectually sharp, capable, and agile. (10%)

- **Interpersonal Savvy:** Relates well to all kinds of people: up, down, and sideways, inside and outside the organization; builds appropriate rapport; listens; builds constructive and effective relationships; uses diplomacy and tact; truly values people. (45%)

- **Lifelong Training and Development:** Coach engages in continual personal and professional development. (62%)

- **Managing Obstacles:** Identify and manage internal and external obstacles. Facilitates anticipating obstacles to their goals, and recognizing if they are internal or external and rehearses potential solutions. (62%)

- **Managing Progress and Accountability:** Ability to hold attention on what is important for the client, and to leave responsibility with the client to take action; clearly requests of the client actions that will move the client toward their stated goals; demonstrates follow through by asking the client about those actions that the client committed to during the previous session(s); acknowledges the client for what they have done, not done, learned or become aware of since the previous coaching session(s); effectively prepares, organizes and reviews with client information obtained during sessions; keeps the client on track between sessions by holding attention on the coaching plan and outcomes, agreed-upon courses of action, and topics for future session(s); focuses on the coaching plan but is also open to adjusting behaviors and actions based on the coaching process and shifts in direction during sessions; is able to move back and forth between the big picture of where the client is heading, setting a context for what is being discussed and where the client wishes to go; promotes client's self-discipline and holds the client accountable for what they say they are going to do, for the results of an intended action, or for a specific plan with related time frames; develops the client's ability to make decisions, address key concerns, and develop himself/ herself (to get feedback, to determine priorities and set the pace of learning, to reflect on and learn from experiences); positively confronts the client with the fact that he/she did not take agreed-upon actions. (66%)

- **Meeting Ethical Guidelines and Professional Standards:** Understanding of coaching ethics and standards and ability to apply them appropriately in all coaching situations; understands and exhibits in own behaviors the ICF standards of conduct: understands and follows all ICF ethical guidelines; clearly communicates the distinctions between coaching, consulting, psychotherapy and other support professions; refers client to another support professional as needed, knowing when this is needed and the available resources. (55%)

- **Planning and Goal Setting:** Ability to develop and maintain an effective coaching plan with the client; consolidates collected information and establishes a coaching plan and development goals with the client that address concerns and major areas for learning and development; creates a plan with results that are attainable, measurable, specific and have target dates; makes plan adjustments as warranted by the coaching process and by changes in the situation; helps the client identify and access different resources for learning (e.g., books, other professionals); identifies and targets early successes that are important to the client. (62%)

- **Political Savvy:** Can maneuver through complex political situations effectively and quietly, is sensitive to how people and organizations function, anticipates where the land mines are and plans his or her approach accordingly, views corporate politics as a necessary part of organizational life and works to adjust to that reality. (17%)

- **Powerful Questioning:** Ability to ask questions that reveal the information needed for maximum benefit to the coaching relationship and the client; asks questions that reflect active listening and an understanding of the client's perspective; asks questions that evoke discovery, insight, commitment or action (e.g., those that challenge the client's assumptions); asks open-ended questions that create greater clarity, possibility or new learning; asks questions that move the client towards what they desire, not questions that ask for the client to justify or look backwards. (83%)

- **Resource Identification:** Coach assists client to identify attainable resources that will enable client to achieve their goal. (31%)
- **Self-Knowledge:** Knows personal strengths, weaknesses, opportunities, and limits; seeks feedback; gains insights from mistakes; is open to criticism; isn't defensive; is receptive to talking about shortcomings. (59%)
- **Thought Partner:** Assists client to think more in-depth, engage in more critical thinking and arrive at better decisions. (66%)
  Use of Assessments: Use a variety of structured and unstructured assessments to assist the Client's self-understanding. (41%)
- **Utilization of Coaching Tools:** Such as the ladder of inference, left-hand column exercise, life satisfaction scales, etc. (28%)
- **Values Identification and Clarification:** Client and coach identify and clarify the client's values as they relate to the client's goal. (38%)

Acknowledgements: I would like to express my appreciation to Jeanne Auerbach, Teri-E. Belf, Maynard Brusman, Diane Foster, Sandra Foster, Ana Maria Irueste-Montes, Pamela McLean, Christine Martin, Andrea Molberg, Relly Nadler, David Peterson, Peter Reding, Pamela Richarde, Robert Voyle and Randy White for their assistance on this project.

 *Jeffrey E. Auerbach, Ph. D., PCC is the founder and president of College of Executive Coaching. The College of Executive Coaching is an ICF Accredited Coach Training Program with courses ongoing worldwide and based in Pismo Beach, California. Jeffrey is the author of Personal and Executive Coaching: The Complete Guide for Mental Health Professionals, the editor of Building Competence in Personal and Executive Coaching, and the research director of the 2005 State of the Coaching Industry Project. He is the Program Committee Co-Chair of the Tenth International Coach Federation Conference, on the Editorial Board of the International Journal of Coaching in Organizations. He earned the ICF Professional Certified Coach (PCC) credential. Dr. Auerbach is a graduate of the University of California, Santa Barbara, the California Graduate Institute and Antioch University and earned a Ph.D. in Psychology. Contact: ja@executivecoachcollege.com*

Evidence-Based Practice:
A Potential Approach for Effective Coaching

Dianne R. Stober
Leni Wildflower
David Drake

As coaching develops as an emerging profession, it is vital for coaches to begin integrating evidence from both coaching-specific research and related disciplines, their own expertise, and an understanding of the uniqueness of each client. Evidence-based practices (EBPs) encompass these three endeavors in designing interventions aimed at positive growth and change for their recipients. While coaching does not have an extensive body of specific knowledge, there is a wealth of evidence from fields such as psychology, adult learning, communication, and others which has a bearing on coaches' knowledge and practice. An EBP approach has the potential to raise the standards of practice and training, increase the credibility of coaching as an intervention, and stretch the individual coach's thinking and practice, if undertaken in its broadest form. However, we suggest there are a number of questions raised by the application of EBP to coaching.

What Is Evidence-Based Practice?

In developing an evidence-based approach to coaching, it is helpful to look at how evidence-based practice has developed and been discussed in other related fields. EBP first grew out of the practice of medicine and has since influenced other fields, notably psychology. It has been a discussion with some controversy, much of which goes to the heart of where research and theory relate to practice and where "artful" practice and "scientific" evidence meet. So first, let us lay out a definition from medicine:

Evidence-based practice is "the conscientious, explicit and judicious use of current best evidence in making decisions about the care of individual patients, [which] means integrating individual clinical expertise with the best available external clinical evidence from systematic research (Sackett, Haynes, Guyatt, and Tugwell, 1996, p. 71).

In unpacking this definition, there are three main characteristics that bear discussion. First, EBP requires that the practitioner (doctor, psychologist, coach, etc.) use the best available knowledge in his or her field. Second, the EBP practitioner needs to integrate this knowledge with his or her own expertise. Third, this integration must be accomplished in the context of each client's individual situation. When these three variables are taken into account, interventions will be uniquely customized for each client using a comprehensive and practical framework.

As such, EBP is not following a rigid protocol to avoid flying by the seat of your pants. It requires a (very) thoughtful approach in evaluating what is known about different techniques, what our experience tells us, and what our client specifically needs in order to achieve success. Practitioners using an evidence-based approach must be able to evaluate theory and research for applicability and utility in their coaching, integrate this knowledge with their own expertise in practice, skillfully weave their approach with their client's needs, values and preferences and, finally, assess their intervention's effectiveness for the client and the coaching relationship.

Best Available Knowledge

In looking at our best available knowledge for evidence, coaching is at a relative disadvantage compared with older professions such as psychology and medicine. At this time, we have very little research specifically evaluating coaching in terms of outcomes, specific techniques, or underlying mechanisms of change in coaching (Stober, 2004; Stober and Parry, 2004; for an annotated bibliography see Grant 2003). Most of our evidence is anecdotal or descriptive. As such, it is a rich source of hypotheses and theory development but does not give us explicit evidence about what "works" in coaching or why it works. However, before there is gnashing of teeth and rending of hair, we should recognize that while coaching as a widespread approach is relatively new, it has roots in a number of fields. Therefore, one of the significant tasks before us is the integration and application of this disparate knowledge base into a coherent body of knowledge that applies to and guides coaching.

For example, most coaches would agree that coaching involves achieving meaningful positive change with clients. There is a large body of research regarding the change process in psychotherapy that can be extrapolated to coaching. The Transtheoretical Model (TTM) is one of the best researched (Prochaska, DiClemente, and Norcross, 1992) and describes a stage model of change that has been demonstrated to describe how individuals move from one behavior to another, more desired behavior. Assessing a client's readiness for change is a prerequisite of effective intervention according to the model. Along these same lines, coaches discuss "coachability," as a prerequisite for changes in their clients; they could benefit from the evidence produced by the TTM research to better understand and promote coachability. We have much work ahead of us in explicitly linking valuable evidence from other disciplines to the development and application of coaching.

What Counts as "Evidence"?

While most coaches would agree that it is best to have evidence for what we do, the question of "what constitutes evidence?" remains. As has been stated, there is little empirical research dealing with the effectiveness or mechanisms of coaching Given the current status of coaching-specific research, at this point in the evolution of coaching as an evidence-based practice, we are mostly left to extrapolate evidence from other disciplines and using the primarily descriptive coaching-specific research to formulate hypotheses and models for further study.

As coaching becomes an intervention subject to increasing scrutiny and research, we have the advantage of learning from the debates within evidence-based movements in other fields. Rather than increasing a division between "researchers" and "practitioners" as has happened in related disciplines (see Stober, 2004 for an argument for a scientist-practitioner model of coaching), coaches can use a broad definition of "evidence" that allows for a variety of research methods.

A number of authors in psychology have eloquently argued against over-valuing nomothetic, controlled quantitative research and ignoring ideographic, qualitative methods (Messer, 2004; Edwards, Dattilio, and Bromley, 2004; Peterson, 1991). Westen, Novotny, and Thompson-Brenner, (2004) question whether tightly controlled clinical trials have enough external validity to apply to general, day-to-day practice. Wampold, Ahn, and Coleman (2001) suggest a medical model of change does not account for outcomes in behavioral change, in this case, through psychotherapy. This is not to say that the randomized clinical trial, the "gold standard" of medical intervention, as a methodology is not useful, but rather to underscore the need to recognize its limits. Systematic case study designs (Edwards, Dattilio, and Bromley, 2004, Messer, 2004), quasi-experimental methods and literature syntheses (McCabe, 2004), and qualitative methods all have their place in accumulating evidence regarding interventions. Building multiple streams of coaching-specific evidence for practical use, rather than relying on one type of evidence, is one necessary step towards a full evidence-based approach.

The emerging profession of coaching has the opportunity to promote the development of complementary research methods directed at building a more fully integrated base of evidence that will be useful and valid for practitioners. Coaches will still need the requisite skills to recognize strengths and limitations of various research methods and to evaluate the appropriateness of applying research evidence to practice.

A related question an evidence-based practitioner must answer for her or himself is at what level should research evidence apply to practice: general principles of change, models of intervention, or specific techniques? Given that much evidence is extrapolations from other fields at this time, evidence-based coaches would do well to first evaluate the evidence's applicability to more general structures in coaching and then begin to adapt it for particular techniques.

Practitioner Expertise

The expertise needed for applying various types of evidence to practice is just as important as the availability of knowledge. Again, drawing parallels from the related discipline of psychology (Crits-Christoph, et al., 1991), we can surmise that the individual coach is a factor related to outcomes. Understanding what coaches do in order to be effective in building coaching relationships, engaging in coaching conversations and achieving coaching results is important—as is explicating how they develop this expertise.

One of the challenges of bringing practitioner expertise to bear in the further development of coaching is the reality that coaches have come to this work from numerous backgrounds (notably business and management, psychology and related disciplines, and education and adult learning), with a wide variety of education and training, and only the loosest of agreements on the definitions of the profession and of what it means to be a professional. Most coaches are applying their skills and knowledge from other fields using structures and techniques they learned in coach training organizations. While many of the programs have a theoretical base, some quite extensive, these training programs are primarily designed to develop coaches as practitioners. We have yet to develop a thorough grounding for training encompassing theory, research, and practice that is coaching-specific.

The International Coach Federation and other organizations have begun defining required coaching competencies—though they are primarily related to practical experience. Research is still needed, however, to evaluate whether the proposed competencies are actually tied to positive outcomes or not. At least for some of these competencies, there is a body of literature that addresses parallel concepts in psychotherapy. For example, a core competency outlined by ICF involves the ability of the coach to establish trust and intimacy with the client. Psychotherapy outcome research has demonstrated the importance of developing a positive relationship between practitioner and client, termed the working alliance (Horvath and Symonds, 1991). These authors define it as encompassing the collaboration between therapist and client and also the capacities of both to negotiate an appropriate contract for the relationship. Drawing a parallel to coaching, what is known about the development of a working alliance in psychotherapy probably has some similar components in coaching, as in the ICF competence regarding Co-Creating the Relationship.

The goal then is to make the connections between coaching and the related research and evidence in a way that has both scientific integrity and practical utility. "Although some revel in it, the very success of the practitioner strains the discipline. To a degree, wherever a discipline contains both basic and applied interests there is tension" (Denmark and Krauss, 2005, p.17). If there is no research-driven foundation for the ongoing development of practitioners and the profession, coaches run the risk of exacerbating this tension. While it is beyond the scope of this discussion to link existing research from related fields to coaching competencies and expertise, it is important to note that such data is available and, should an evidence-based philosophy become adopted by the coaching community, these links will need to be fully explored.

In addition to possessing specified competencies in coaching, an "expert" coach has other qualities that come into play in an evidence-based approach. Experts have a depth and breadth of knowledge which can flexibly be applied to individual clients. As discussed earlier, in order to practice at the highest level, experts must apply the best available evidence for each individual client. Doing this fluidly requires high interpersonal skill on the part of the coach. Experts also recognize when the limits of their knowledge and expertise have been reached and do not practice beyond their skill. By "owning" their knowledge and recognizing their limits, expert coaches also engage in self-reflection and continuing education.

Evidence-based practice requires that the individual coach parlay their expertise and available knowledge into an exquisite tool to be used in individual scenarios. Since research evidence often may not fit their unique, individual coaching engagements, the coach must rely on their own expertise and judgment to select and customize the methods employed. This requires, in turn, a deep understanding of the client, bringing us to the third component of EBP.

Client Characteristics

It is not sufficient to evaluate specific techniques or interventions or to implement expertise regarding relationships without also taking into account the client's particular nature, situation and goals. Our clients' worldviews, expectations, and values are all as central to effective coaching as any particular intervention or the relationship between coach and client. What the client brings to the relationship has direct bearing on whether and how coaching will progress.

One of the main issues in taking clients' contexts into account is the dilemma of trying to devise techniques and build a body of data that can apply to an aggregate of clients and also handle individual differences. Most quantitative research strives for internal validity to allow for rigorous testing and is thus susceptible to limited generalizability beyond the sample studied. Many qualitative methods give rich contextual and individual descriptions but generally do not enable us to explain or predict behavior change. In an evidence-based approach, coach practitioners and those designing coaching research will need to draw on multiple sources of evidence that can be evaluated for use with each unique client. Coaches using EBP need to take into account an array of variables the make up the individual context of each client, including age, developmental and life stages, sociocultural contexts (e.g., gender, culture, socioeconomic status, religious beliefs, etc.), current environmental factors (e.g., career and employment status, networks of communities, levels of stress, etc.), individual and personality factors (e.g., readiness for change, resilience, interpersonal styles, worldviews, self-schemas, etc.), and individual expectations for the coaching. Coaching-specific research is needed regarding who best benefits (and who does not) from coaching and what characteristics they share. Psychological research regarding some of these variables exists and, again, there is a need for linking this body of knowledge with what can be extrapolated to coaching. Overall, being able to use available knowledge with one's expertise is most effective when matched with the individual client in a particular coaching engagement.

Should EBP be Applied to Coaching?

This discussion has aimed to describe how an evidence-based approach might be used in the development of coaching. Given that description, a number of questions are raised:

1. Is there enough evidence at this point that can be tied to coaching?
2. Who gets to decide what counts as evidence?
3. What types of evidence should be developed and how should they be weighted?
4. If coaching adopts EBP as a desired model, how can we avoid the overvaluing of one type of research evidence over another?
5. How, and at what level of specificity of application, should research evidence be translated to coaching practice?
6. How would coach training and education have to shift in order to support coaching as an EBP?
7. If EBP is adopted, how do we balance the need for accountability in using evidence-based interventions with further innovation and exploration of potentially effective techniques and methods?

8. Will an adoption of EBP methods be used by other stakeholders (e.g., organizations paying for coaching, regulatory agencies) for an increase in quality and credibility of coaching or to limit choices available for coaches and clients?

Evidence-based practice holds much promise as an approach to increase the credibility and quality of coaching. By learning from the experience of other fields in exploring evidence-based practices, coaching may fashion an integrated, comprehensive approach to the most effective interventions. There remains much discussion beyond this article to help flesh out both the possible benefits and the potential pitfalls of such an approach.

Summary

In describing an evidence-based practice approach to coaching, parallels have been drawn from other fields' experience. Use of the best available knowledge, the practitioner's expertise, and taking into account client preferences are the three primary ingredients that make up the concept of an evidence-based practice. In order to avoid the confounding of EBP with any one type of evidence, it is paramount to stress the importance of multiple streams of evidence in translating science into practice, as no one type of data or methodology can give us a complete picture of what is effective. There is a wealth of evidence across a variety of fields that can be extrapolated to coaching and expanded upon in coaching-specific research.

In addition, identifying and developing the practitioner's expertise in evaluating and applying the best available knowledge is important for the coaching community and for the individual coach working with individual clients. Evaluating known evidence regarding practitioner expertise in other fields will enable us to design research that will confirm, add to, modify, or disconfirm competencies already proposed for coaching. And finally, the integration of the best evidence with an expert practitioner is useless without taking into account the individual client and their context.

As coaching professionals design methodologies based on these concepts: 1) best available knowledge, 2) practitioner expertise, and 3) client preferences, we will build an independent body of coaching research, practice, and data that will not only build a body of practical experience that is verifiable as effective coaching, but as a profession, we will stand firm among the other disciplines in the academic canon..

References

Crits-Christoph, P., Baranackie, K., Kurcias, J. S., Carroll, K., Luborsky, L., McLellan, T., et al. (1991). Meta-analysis of therapist effects in psychotherapy outcome studies. *Psychotherapy Research, 1,* 81-91.

Denmark, F., & Krauss, H. K. (2005). Unification through diversity. In R. J. Sternberg (Ed.), *Unity in psychology: Possibility or pipe dream?* (pp. 15-36). Washington, DC: American Psychological Association.

Edwards, D. J. A., Dattilio, F. M., & Bromley, D. B. (2004). Developing evidence-based practice: The role of case-based research. *Professional Psychology: Research and Practice, 35,* 589-597.

Grant, A.M. (2003). Keeping up with the cheese! Research as a foundation for professional coaching of the future. In I. F. Stein and L. A. Belsten (Eds.), *Proceedings of the 1st ICF Coaching Research Symposium,* 1-19. Mooresville, NC: Paw Print Press.

Horvath, A. O., & Symonds, B. D. (1991). Relation between working alliance and outcome in psychotherapy. *Journal of Counseling Psychology, 38,* 139-149.

McCabe, O. L. (2004). Crossing the quality chasm in behavioral health care: The role of evidence-based practice. *Professional Psychology: Research and Practice, 35,* 571-579.

Messer, S. B. (2004). Evidence-based practice: Beyond empirically supported treatments. *Professional Psychology: Research and Practice, 35,* 580-588.

Peterson, D. R. (1991). Connection and disconnection of research and practice in the education of professional psychologists. *American Psychologist, 46,* 422-429.

Prochaska, J. O., DiClemente, C. C., Norcross, J. C. (1992). In search of how people change. *American Psychologist, 47,* 1102-1114.

Sackett, D. L., Haynes, R. B., Guyatt, G. H., & Tugwell, P. (1996). Evidence based medicine: What it is and what it isn't. *British Medical Journal, 13,* 71-72.

Stober, D.R. (2005). Coaching eye for the research guy and research eye for the coaching guy: 20/20 vision for coaching through the scientist-practitioner model. In I. F. Stein, F. Campone, & L. J. Page (Eds.), *Proceedings of the 2nd ICF Coaching Research Symposium,* 13-21. Washington, DC: International Coach Federation.

Stober, D. R. & Parry, C. (2004). Current challenges and future directions in coaching research. In A. M. Grant, M. J. Cavanagh, & T. Kemp, *Evidence-based coaching (Vol. 1): Contributions from the Behavioral Sciences.* Sydney, Australia: Australian Academic Press.

Wampold, B. E., Ahn, H., & Coleman, H. L. K. (2001). Medical model as metaphor: Old habits die hard. *Journal of Counseling Psychology, 48,* 268-273.

Westen, D., Novotny, C., & Thompson-Brenner, H. (2004). Empirical status of empirically supported psychotherapies: Assumptions, findings, and reporting in controlled clinical trials. *Psychological Bulletin, 130,* 631-663.

Dianne Stober, Ph.D., is a leader in developing theoretical and empirical foundations for coaching practice. She is a faculty member in the Organizational Management and Organizational Development master's program at Fielding Graduate University. Along with her colleagues at Fielding, Dianne also teaches in the new Evidence-Based Coaching Certificate Program. Dianne is currently co-editing The Evidence-Based Coaching Handbook (Wiley, due out early 2006). An academic and a practitioner, she has presented and published her work in a wide variety of scholarly and professional venues such as the ICF, the American Psychological Association, the Professional Coach and Mentor Association, the Australian Evidence-Based Coaching Conference, and the International Journal of Coaching in Organizations. Dr. Stober maintains an active coaching practice working with individuals and organizations. She received her Ph.D. in clinical psychology from Georgia State University, completed her internship at the University of Colorado Health Sciences Center, and a postdoctoral fellowship at Emory University. Contact: dstober@fielding.edu.

Leni Wildflowr, Ph.D., has worked for thirty years in the field of organization development, coaching, and human relations, designing programs and interventions for schools, businesses and non-profit agencies. She is a faculty member in the Organizational Management and Organizational Development master's program at Fielding Graduate University where she teaches coaching and conflict resolution courses. Dr. Wildflower directs and teaches in the Evidence-Based Coaching Certificate Program at Fielding. She has written curricula, conducted trainings, and designed coaching interventions for organizations including The Rand Corporation, Santa Monica Hospital Rape Treatment Center, the Center for Creative Leadership, the Conrad Hilton Foundation, US Investigations Service, BP, and First Data Corporation. A graduate of UC Berkeley, she earned a Masters degree from the University of Hawaii in Health Management and a Doctorate from the Fielding Graduate Institute in Human and Organizational Development. Contact: lwildflower@fielding.edu.

David Drake, Ph.D., has twenty years of experience supporting change projects, management and leadership development, and coaching initiatives in over seventy organizations. Dr. Drake has a particular interest in the power of stories to transform people and organizations. He coaches people who want to improve how they lead change, projects, teams or their own life. He has developed extensive training resources on coaching skills in the workplace and taught his coaching skills program. He has helped organizations to move to a coaching-based culture and performance system. Dr. Drake is launching the field of narrative coaching through his new institute. He is active in the international coaching research community and has written/co-written ten papers on theories and methods for the transformative use of stories in coaching, a model for the development of mastery in coaches, and a framework for coaching as an evidence-based practice. He earned a doctorate in Human and Organizational Systems from Fielding Graduate University. Contact: ddrake@narrativecoaching.com.

Relational Flow:
A Theoretical Model for the Intuitive Dance

Margaret Moore
David Drake
Bob Tschannen-Moran
Francine Campone
Carol Kauffman

Inspired by participant comments at the ICF 2004 Coaching Research Symposium, the authors of this paper have collaborated to develop a theoretical model for the intuitive dance, a widely used coaching concept that is not well-defined or well-understood. We are positioning the model as part of a theory-building process to deepen the understanding of mastery in coaching and further the development of an academic foundation for the profession.

The authors define the intuitive dance as a relational dynamic between coaches and clients when they enter a zone where they are fully challenged at a high level of skill and awareness. At those peak moments the coach and the client are in a state we describe as relational flow. Relational flow extends the theory of flow (Csikszentmihalyi, 1990, 1993, 1997, 2000) and builds on Csikszentmihalyi's (Csikszentmihalyi and Csikszentmihalyi, 1988; Csikszentmihalyi and Larson, 1984) notion of shared flow by emphasizing the relational genesis of this state.

In order to explain the relational dynamics of the intuitive dance and build a theoretical model to support further research and development, it is important to draw on other related theories. In this paper, we provide an overview of flow theory in addition to introducing four others that contribute to the emergence of relational flow in coaching:

1. Reflective practitioner (Schön, 1983)
2. Readiness to change (Prochaska, Norcross, and DiClemente, 1995)
3. Emotional intelligence (Goleman, 1995, 1998)
4. Relational competence (Miller, 2004)

The use of relational flow as a theoretical model for studying the practice of coaching will help to understand and promote mastery in the profession. This emerging body of work highlights the importance of the coaching relationship as a vehicle for flow states, growth, and change. We offer examples of additional research that will build on and further this model.

Rationale for Theory-building for the Intuitive Dance

The development of an academic foundation is an important endeavor if coaching is to evolve as a profession. An important element in the process is to identify and study concepts that express the uniqueness of coaching and offer the potential for sound theories and bases for outcomes research. We have identified the intuitive dance as such a concept. Many coaches speak of their peak coaching interactions as an intuitive dance, but a robust and coherent understanding of this phenomenon and its implications is lacking.

We propose that the development of a theoretical model is the first step in a theory-building process for the intuitive dance in coaching. We draw on a definition of theory as a coherent description, explanation, and representation of observed or experienced phenomena (Gioia and Pitre, 1990). Theory-building is the recurring process by which these phenomena are generated, verified, and refined (Lynham, 2000).

There are two primary outcomes from this process according to Dubin (1976): outcome knowledge that is explanatory and predictive in nature and process knowledge that increase the understanding of how something works. As Grant (2005) observed, a good theory accurately describes the part of the world under study, and it is able to guide actions and predict outcomes. Good theories also add to the knowledge base that serves as the foundation for the development and evaluation of a field's practice (Chalofsky, 1996).

So, given that a good theory about the relational dynamic in coaching would deliver important outcomes for the coaching field, we have developed relational flow as a theoretical model for the intuitive dance and outlined directions for future research. We propose that the development and study of a theoretical model for the intuitive dance may:(a) explain why masterful coaches get better results with their clients, (b) provide a basis for coaching outcome studies, (c) provide a roadmap for the development of mastery in coaching, and (d) demonstrate a process for developing theories and studying other coaching concepts.

Proposed Definition of the Intuitive Dance

The intuitive dance is a relational dynamic between coaches and clients when they enter a zone where they are fully challenged at a high level of skill and awareness. The shift into this state can arise from the coach, the client, or the "field" within which the coaching conversation occurs. This dynamic, which we conceptualized as relational flow, may underpin how and when both coaches and their clients make large steps forward in their work.

Relational flow is "intuitive" in that it fosters an awareness of not only what can be observed and discovered empirically but also of what can be directly experienced. It is a "dance" in that it moves through many steps that can be progressively learned and ultimately mastered. This combination uniquely describes a relational process that both deepens the levels of interaction and accelerates the potential for better outcomes.

By way of analogy, coaching conversations are to coaching outcomes as dance classes are to dancing. Over time, the initial mechanical consideration of sequential or rote steps is transformed into a more fluid and situational application of expertise. This shift can be observed in the coaching conversations and their outcomes for both the client and the coach. The coach's mastery of core coaching competencies sets the stage for moments of relational flow when self-consciousness is transcended and new discoveries emerge.

Similar to the experience of being happy, being in relational flow within a coaching session is something both participants know is happening but can be hard pressed to describe or define. It happens when a coach and his or her client perceive themselves as being "in synch" and engaged in a generative, interdependent dialogue. The relational flow model provides a structure to study and advance coaching by: (a) understanding coaching processes and contexts that foster flow; and (b) helping coaches and clients find flow more readily and often (Nakamura and Csikszentmihalyi, 2002).

As Csikszentmihalyi's model (discussed below) would suggest, intuitive dancing is more the exception than the rule. Even so, coaches aspire to the dance during every coaching conversation and masterful coaches dance more often with their clients than novice coaches and achieve greater results in and beyond the coaching sessions.

Relevant Theories to the Intuitive Dance

The core body of knowledge upon which we base our understanding of the intuitive dance is the research of Mihaly Csikszentmihalyi on the experience of flow (1990, 1993, 1997, 2000) and, in particular, his (Csikszentmihalyi and Csikszentmihalyi, 1988; Csikszentmihalyi and Larson, 1984) notion of shared flow as distinguishable from optimal individual experience in group settings where the others may or may not be in flow. We have also identified four theories that support our theoretical model. They can be framed within a grid defined by inner versus outer foci and interpersonal versus intrapersonal processes and they contribute to a better understanding of the dynamics of relational flow as it emerges at certain moments in coaching conversations. These theories further help position relational flow as an integral part of masterful coaching and as a theoretical model to guide research and practitioner development. The four theories are:

1. Reflective Practitioner (Schön, 1983): The coach draws on his or her mastery of coaching competencies and knowledge derived from prior experiences to construct original and spontaneous responses to what the client brings to the interaction.
2. Readiness to Change (Prochaska et al, 1995): The coach and client both have the cognitive and emotional foundation that is a prerequisite for embarking on and completing a path of change.
3. Emotional Intelligence (Goleman, 1995, 1998): The coach and client have high levels of emotional intelligence, including awareness and abilities to manage, express, and leverage emotions within relationships.
4. Relational Competence (Miller, 2004; Walker and Rosen, 2004): The coach and client are competent in growth-promoting relationships that foster psychological development through deeper connections.

Taking a multiparadigmatic view of this phenomenon is more representative of the multifaceted nature of the individual and relational realities in coaching conversations (Gioia and Pitre, 1990). In the end, the ultimate judge of whether or not the proposed model has yielded a good theory will be found in the application of resulting practices by coaches (Lynham, 2000).

In Exhibit 1, the theoretical model of the intuitive dance is overlaid on an adapted version of Wilber's (2000) "All-Quadrant" model to show how these additional theories support relational flow.

Exhibit 1: <u>Relational Flow: Theoretical Model for Intuitive Dance</u>

OUTER	Reflective practitioner	Relational Flow	Relational competence
INNER	Readiness to change		Emotional intelligence
	INTRAPERSONAL		INTERPERSONAL

Flow

For more than 30 years, Mihaly Csikszentmihalyi has involved thousands of subjects in both qualitative and quantitative research to characterize flow as the psychology of optimal experience. Flow is the experience people have when they are completely immersed in an activity for its own sake, stretching body and mind to the limit in a voluntary effort to accomplish something difficult and worthwhile (Csikszentmihalyi, 1997). It is used by many people to describe "the sense of effortless action they feel in moments that stand out as the best in their lives. Athletes refer to it as 'being in the zone'" (Csikszentmihalyi, 1997, p. 29). The flow experience expands an individual's goal and interest structure and the skills relevant to an existing interest (Nakamura and Csikszentmihalyi, 2002). Flow also often involves the anticipation of desired future states which becomes a prolepsis that can be as engaging as actually reaching those states. One good example is the use of pre-event visualization exercises by elite athletes.

Coaches seek to foster the flow state in clients; our hypothesis is that flow is co-created within the relational dynamic when certain conditions are present. Our theoretical model offers a structure to identify and study those conditions and their implications.

Exhibit 2: <u>Finding Flow</u>

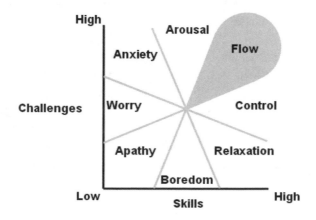

Csikszentmihalyi (2000) initially portrayed flow as a "channel" that represents an optimal balance between one's perceived abilities and the perceived challenge at a high enough level to avoid both boredom (too much skill for the challenge) and anxiety (too much challenge for the skill). In flow, as represented by a later diagram similar to the example in Exhibit 2, an individual is engaged in a challenging situation that requires fully engaging and stretching one's skills at a high level in response. It enables a person to paradoxically be engaged fully in the experience for itself and yet achieve optimal outcomes.

The relational dynamic in coaching offers cues for the coach in deciding what action to take next. Sometimes these cues are explicitly stated; other times they are intuitively inferred: Is the client in control, but not yet in flow? Then perhaps the dance needs to become more challenging. Is the client aroused, but not yet in flow? Then perhaps the dancers need to become more competent or aware.

So what are the characteristics of a flow experience? They include: clear proximal goals, decisiveness, merger of action and awareness, complete (yet effortless) concentration, sense of control, loss of self-consciousness, altered sense of time, immediate feedback, and an autotelic emphasis (Csikszentmihalyi, 1993; Nakamura and Csikszentmihalyi, 2002). Flow research has historically emphasized the dynamic system composed of the person and his or her environment, as well as the phenomenology of person-environment interactions (Nakamura and Csikszentmihalyi, 2002). As flow states unfold, what happens in any moment is a response to what happened immediately before, rather than being dictated by a preexisting intentional structure in the person or the environment (Nakamura and Csikszentmihalyi, 2002).

This is where our concept of the intuitive dance as relational flow goes beyond Csikszentmihalyi's model. Whereas Csikszentmihalyi writes of finding flow in primarily individual terms, the intuitive dance builds more on his notion of shared flow to suggest that relational flow is a co-created experience emerging from the relational dynamic of the coaching conversation. When the coach and the client are fully challenged at a high level of skill and awareness in a co-creative partnership, relational flow is generated and the potential for clients to make desired changes is enhanced. In fact, both coach and client are often changed by the intuitive dance and move forward developmentally as a result.

A second difference between flow and relational flow is that the former focuses on the autotelic nature of the experience as an end to itself whereas the latter is embedded within a coaching partnership in which outcomes are anticipated and expected.

What are the conditions that foster relational flow and hence contribute to it as a theoretical model? The first condition is a coach who has developed professional mastery. Second, the client needs to be ready to change and able to step into flow with the coach. Third, both coach and client need to have a high level of emotional intelligence and relational competence to be able to use the conversations, the partnership, and the field or "third area" (Schwartz-Salant, 1986, 1998; Drake, 2005) created in their sessions. Hence, we propose that these four theories contribute to relational flow in coaching as represented in our theoretical model.

Reflective Practitioner

How is it that some coaches are able to enter into relational flow with their clients more easily and often than others? One of the key variables is the coach's level of professional mastery. Relational flow is predicated on the coach's mastery of the core competencies of coaching and the resulting ability to reflect in action by engaging in a continual process of rapid feedback and adjustment (Jackson, 2004). Research into mastery in coaching is important because experts work with knowledge differently than do novices. A master is a professional who is less tied to explicit rules, processes, and contextual cues in order to know how to act effectively — and yet does so with less effort. Experts are able to use the limited capacity of working memory to greater advantage than can novices, who must draw on it regularly to navigate client situations.

Experts do this by using their long-term memory schemata as the basis for the representation and resolution of problems. Through experience, and the deeper and broader knowledge that is then possible, experts direct their attention to the features of the case that are most associated with the problem diagnosis and therefore can quickly narrow the problem space (Clark, 1999). We hypothesize that this, in part, is what enables a coach to tune out distractions and consciously or unconsciously tune into the coaching moment in ways that can lead to the intuitive dance.

In Schön's (1983) research on reflective practice, mastery can be seen as the ability to draw on one's experience and expertise to recognize patterns, discern any incongruities between the pattern and the situation, reflect on what is discovered, and develop a new pattern of response to address the needs at hand. When we reflect, we shift from pattern thinking to meta-cognitive awareness. It may be that this level of awareness is tied to the presence of relational flow and the transcendence of the initial patterns brought to coaching conversations by both clients and coaches. Patterns give way, through reflective listening, to "not in pattern," which make possible new patterns. When a coach and client enter into relational flow it can be seen as crossing a threshold beyond the patterns with which they began (Drake, 2005), a process often marked with both risk and exhilaration. In keeping within Exhibit 2, we propose that reflective practice exemplifies the process of managing and developing one's intrapersonal state in relation with one's actions and environment.

Reflective practice contributes to relational flow as a way to describe how coaches move between thinking and non-thinking, analysis and reflection. Masterful practitioners have learned to do this with greater ease as they move between the patterns they recognize and the emergent needs of the moment in order to create and sustain relational flow with their clients. This is much like the use of intuition by a chess master. Years of practice culminate in actions, which appear to be effortless playing. As Daniel Kahneman (2002) notices, however, intuition as used by a master chess player and a new pupil are not the same thing. We suggest that it is for masterful coaches who are able to engage in continual cycles of feedback and adaptation.

Readiness to Change

Prochaska's (1995) trans-theoretical model defines a set of building blocks necessary for lasting change in behavior and self-concept. We propose that four of these building blocks for change contribute to a client's ability to engage in relational flow and a coach's ability to co-create this dance. Mastery in coaching requires an ability to assess clients' readiness and effectively apply the appropriate strategies to help them move forward. Relational flow may be both an outcome of and a contributor to the increased presence of these characteristics in the coaching relationship. It is striking to note that they bear a strong resemblance to Csikszentmihalyi's (1990, 1993, 1997) notion of the autotelic self. The four building blocks are:

1. *Raised Consciousness:* Awareness of the good and bad consequences of both the status quo and future possibilities, including change in goals, mental models, behavior, relationships, and self-image.
2. *Self-Awareness:* Conscious recognition of one's own patterns, strengths, weaknesses, and deepest desires including the desire to increase self-awareness.
3. *Self-Reevaluation:* An attitude of welcoming and enjoying curious and empathic inquiry and reflections on current situations and future potential.
4. *Emotional Arousal:* Access to the emotional energy which sparks motivation and supports resolve.

This theory offers a way to help clients assess their own intrapersonal state in terms of their ability to actually make the changes they desire and declare. An effective coaching partnership incorporates these building blocks of change as they are needed in response to the client's readiness for change. Masterful coaches ask themselves, "What does my client need most right now?" It may be that moments of relational flow signal and facilitate a shift in a client's development or self-concept and in their ability to make sustainable change.

Emotional Intelligence

Relational flow demands a high level of emotional awareness from both the coach and the client. Emotional intelligence, the signature work of Daniel Goleman (1995, 1998), provides an excellent framework for understanding and developing this awareness. It refers to the capacity for "recognizing our own feelings and those of others, for motivating ourselves, and for managing emotions well in ourselves and in our relationships" (Goleman, 1998, p. 317).

Goleman's work has identified five basic emotional and social competencies for emotional intelligence: self-awareness, self-regulation, motivation, empathy, and social skills. Goleman's study of emotional intelligence also recognizes intuition as a form of intelligence suitable for study. Moreover, Goleman contributes to the study of the intuitive dance in human relationships. Those who have low emotional intelligence rarely do the intuitive dance or experience relational flow. How do we increase our emotional intelligence? Goleman describes a 14-step process including assessment, communication, motivation, goal-setting, feedback, practice, support, emulation, environmental modification, and reinforcement.

This process reflects the best practices in coaching, as Goleman (1998) himself acknowledges when he notes that coaching is an increasingly common strategy to boost emotional competence. Emotional intelligence aligns with our theoretical model in providing language and a body of work about the inner abilities of coaches and clients to manage their interpersonal relations in coaching such that moments of relational flow are possible.

Relational Competence

The interpersonal nature of the intuitive dance suggests that a developmental theory about relationships would contribute to our theoretical model. Coaches and clients who are skilled at using relationships to support growth and change will be better intuitive dancers. Relational Cultural Theory (Miller, 2004) is predicated on the belief that people grow through and toward connection and not (just) separation. There is a mutual empathy and overall relational competence that is therefore necessary to support other people's development through and in relationships.

The five qualities of growth-promoting relationships and relational competence from this theory align well with our understanding of relational flow:

1. *Zest:* In connection, each person feels more vitality and can dance energetically. Action: In connection, each person feels more able to act, both within the relationship and beyond it. That occurs both in the here and now interplay of coaching and afterwards, as clients and coaches alike feel more empowered in the world.
2. *Knowledge:* In connection, each person expands awareness of both themselves and the other. The picture is clearer, more objective, and more fully articulated, particularly as the context of connection decreases judgmental attitudes.
3. *Sense of Worth:* In connection, each person feels a greater sense of worth due to the genuine responsiveness of the other as seen in listening and recognition.
4. *Motivation for More Connections:* Being in connection with one party motivates a desire to be fully and deeply connected with others as it instills relational optimism and efficacy.

This body of work speaks to the outer dynamics involved in navigating interpersonal relations in coaching and provides some initial insights into the nature of what masterful coaches do when they move into relational flow with their clients. This process is often aided in coaching by attention to developing a client's skills at moving out of habitual patterns to engage in the present moment more fully and ably.

Next Steps

We have provided an initial theoretical model for the intuitive dance, which we call relational flow. This is the first step in a theory-building process intended to add to the knowledge base for coaching as a profession and field of study as well as inform those who seek mastery in the art of coaching. We will pursue an iterative process based on feedback and collaboration with other practitioners and researchers to further the development of the relational flow model and its theoretical foundation. Possible next steps include refining our understanding of the nature and characteristics of relational flow by testing the model against demonstrations of the intuitive dance by masterful coaches. Other elements of validating a theoretical model include, "interpreting new data, responding to new problems, defining applied problems, evaluating solutions, discerning priorities, identifying new research directions, developing common language and defining boundaries, and guiding and informing research" (Torraco as cited in Lynham1997).

As our theory stabilizes, additional research projects can be conducted, for example:

(a) *Outcome studies* to assess the degree to which increased relational flow leads to better and/or expedited outcomes for clients.

(b) *Mastery and skills-building studies* to define and test the characteristics of relational flow and measure both their use and their relationship to client change.

(c) *Professional development studies* that compare various approaches to developing coaches in terms of the skills needed to move into relational flow.

(d) *Phenomenological studies* to understand the experiences of coaches and clients just before, during, and after periods of relational flow.

(e) *Qualitative studies* to understand what contributes to the emergence of moments of intuitive dancing and what impedes them from happening.

(f) *Quantitative studies* including the development and testing of statistical assessment tools for measuring and evaluating the intuitive dance and its coaching outcomes

(g) *Narrative studies* to explore how coaches and clients narrate the experience of relational flow and what happens with their stories and self-concepts as a result.

(h) *Discourse analysis studies* to examine the role and use of language in periods of relational flow and the transitions in and out of this state.

Conclusions

In conclusion, relational flow is an important theoretical model for coaching that is worthy of further refinement and research. Bringing together five different yet overlapping theories and bodies of work (Flow, Reflective Practitioner, Readiness to Change, Emotional Intelligence, and Relational Competence) enables scholars to more holistically study the intuitive dance as the basis for masterful coaching and as part of an academic foundation for the coaching profession. We believe that relational flow as a theoretical model makes an important contribution to our field as a description of what happens in masterful coaching, and it has the potential to enhance the understanding of how masterful coaching facilitates client growth and change.

References

Clark, R. C. (1999). *Building expertise: Cognitive methods for training and performance improvement.* Washington, DC: International Society for Performance Improvement.

Chalofsky, N. E. (1996). Professionalization comes from theory and research" the "why" instead of the "how to". In R. W. Rowden (Ed.), *Workplace learning: Debating five critical questions of theory and practice* (Vol. 72, pp. 51-56). San Francisco, CA: Jossey-Bass.

Csikszentmihalyi, M. (1990). *Flow: The psychology of optimal experience.* New York, NY: Harper & Row.

Csikszentmihalyi, M. (1993). *The evolving self: A psychology for the third millennium.* New York, NY: Harper Perennial.

Csikszentmihalyi, M. (1997). *Finding flow: The psychology of engagement with everyday life.* New York, NY: Basic Books.

Csikszentmihalyi, M. (2000). *Beyond boredom and anxiety.* San Francisco: Jossey-Bass.

Csikszentmihalyi, M., & Csikszentmihalyi, I. (Eds.). (1988). *Optimal experience.* Cambridge, England: Cambridge University Press.

Csikszentmihalyi, M., & Larson, R. (1984). *Being adolescent.* New York, NY: Basic Books.

Drake, D. B. (2005). Creating third spaces: The use of narrative liminality in organizational coaching. Paper presented at the Western States Communication Association Convention, San Francisco.

Dubin, R. (1976). Theory building in applied areas. In M. D. Dunnette (Ed.), *Handbook of industrial and organizational psychology* (pp. 17-39). Skokie, IL: Rand McNally.

Gioia, D. A., & Pitre, E. (1990). Multiparadigm perspective on theory building. *The Academy of Management Review, 15* (4), 584-602.

Goleman, D. (1995). *Emotional intelligence.* New York: Bantam Books.

Goleman, D. (1998). *Working with emotional intelligence.* New York, NY: Bantam Books.

Jackson, P. (2004). Understanding the experience of experience: A practical model of reflective practice for coaching. *International Journal of Evidence-based Coaching and Mentoring, 2* (1), 57-67.

Grant, A. M. (2005). Introduction. In M. Cavanaugh, A. M. Grant & T. Kemp (Eds.), *Evidence-based coaching: Theory, research and practice from the behavioral sciences (Vol. 1).* Bowen Hills, Qld, Australia: Australian Academic Press.

Jackson, P. (2004). Understanding the experience of experience: A practical model of reflective practice for coaching. *International Journal of Evidence-based Coaching and Mentoring, 2* (1), 57-67.

Kahneman, D. (2002). Maps of bounded rationality: A perspective on intuitive judgment and choice. In T. Frangsmyr (Ed.), *Les prix nobel 2002,* (pp. 416-499).

Lynham, S. A. (2000). Theory building in the human resource development profession. *Human Resource Development Quarterly, 11* (2), 159-178.

Miller, J. B. (2004). What do we mean by relationships. In M. Walker & W. B. Rosen (Eds.), *How connections heal: Stories from relational-cultural therapy.* New York, NY: Guilford Press.

Nakamura, J. & Csikszentmihalyi, M. (2002). The concept of flow. In C. R. Snyder & S. J. Lopezs (Eds.), *Handbook of positive psychology* (pp. 89-105). New York, NY: Oxford University Press.

Prochaska, J. O., Norcross, J., & DiClemente, C. (1995). *Changing for good.* New York, NY: Perennial Currents.

Schön, D. A. (1983). *The reflective practitioner: How professionals think in action.* New York: Basic Books.

Schwartz-Salant, N. (1986). On the subtle-body concept in clinical practice. In N. Schwartz-Salant & M. Stein (Eds.), *The body in analysis.* Wilmette, IL: Chiron Publications.

Schwartz-Salant, N. (1998). *The mystery of human relationship: Alchemy and the transformation of the self.* New York, NY: Routledge.

Torraco, R. J. (1997). Theory-building research methods. In R. A. Swanson & E. F. Holton III (Eds.), *Human resource development handbook: Linking research and practice* (pp. 114-137). San Francisco, CA: Berrett-Koehler.

Wilber, K. (2000). *A theory of everything: An integral vision for business, politics, science and spirituality.* Boston, MA: Shambhala.

Margaret Moore founded Wellcoaches Corporation in 2000. She is the chief architect of the Wellcoaches vision, health, fitness, and wellness coach training and certification programs, and web coaching/coach training platforms. She is an entrepreneur and 17-year veteran of the biotechnology industry in the UK, France, Canada, and the USA. Margaret served in executive roles in two multinational pharmaceutical companies, and as CEO or COO of two startup biotechnology companies, including a cancer biotechnology company. Margaret is the lead author of a Harvard Medical School online CME program titled "Prescribing Lifestyle Medicine for Weight Management" and a new health, fitness, and wellness coach training manual to be published by Lippincott, Williams, & Wilkins. She published a paper in the ICF's 2004 Coaching Research Symposium Proceedings: Principles of Behavioral Psychology in Wellness Coaching. Contact: margaret@wellcoaches.com.

David Drake, Ph.D., has twenty years of experience supporting change projects, management and leadership development, and coaching initiatives in over seventy organizations. Dr. Drake has a particular interest in the power of stories to transform people and organizations. He coaches people who want to improve how they lead change, projects, teams or their own life. He has developed extensive training resources on coaching skills in the workplace and taught his coaching skills program. He has helped organizations to move to a coaching-based culture and performance system. Dr. Drake is launching the field of narrative coaching through his new institute. He is active in the international coaching research community and has written/co-written ten papers on theories and methods for the transformative use of stories in coaching, a model for the development of mastery in coaches, and a framework for coaching as an evidence-based practice. He earned a doctorate in Human and Organizational Systems from Fielding Graduate University. Contact: ddrake@narrativecoaching.com.

Bob Tschannen-Moran is the founder and president of LifeTrek Coaching International. Before founding LifeTrek in 1998, Bob served as a United Church of Christ pastor for 20 years. Bob coached hundreds of people to higher levels of success and fulfillment in life and work. In addition to serving as a mentor coach to aspiring coaches, Bob has worked with business executives and directors, medical doctors, educational leaders, local pastors, and many others. He writes and edits LifeTrek Provisions, a weekly electronic newsletter. Bob received an undergraduate degree from Northwestern University, a Master of Divinity degree from Yale Divinity School, and coach training from Coach U, CoachVille, the Graduate School of Coaching, and Wellcoaches Corporation. In 2005, Bob qualified for certification with both the International Association of Coaches and Wellcoaches Corporation. Contact: Coach@LifeTrekCoaching.com.

Francine Campone, Ed.D., PCC served as a university counselor, faculty member and Associate Dean of Students over the course of a twenty-nine year career. She earned her doctorate in Higher and Adult Education from Columbia University. She earned the International Coach Federation's Professional Certified Coach (PCC) designation. Training in humanistic mediation, group dynamics and facilitation, and Constructive Living Practice complements her coach training. Francine works extensively with leaders of education and nonprofit organizations, and with individuals and teams facing in significant transitions. A founding faculty member of the School of Management's graduate coaching certification program at the University of Texas at Dallas, Francine developed and teaches a course in research for coaches. Dr. Campone was co-editor of the Proceedings of the 2004 ICF Research Symposium and is a member of the leadership team for the 2005 Symposium as well as co-editor of this year's Proceedings. Contact: fcampone@rushmore.com.

Carol Kauffman, Ph.D., ABPP is an Assistant Clinical Professor at Harvard Medical School where she teaches Positive Psychology and introduction to Life Coaching at McLean Hospital. Her book, Pivot Points: Small Choices with the Power to Change Your Life, will be published in 2006. Her work includes "Positive Psychology: The Science at the Heart of Coaching" in Grant and Stober's (2006) book Evidence Based Coaching and "Toward a Positive Psychology of Executive Coaching" in Linley and Joseph's (2004) book Positive Psychology in Practice. Contact: Carol@CarolKauffman.com.

The Ideological Foundations of the Adaptive Coaching Model: A Research-Based Approach To Improving Coaching Results

Terry Bacon

What goes wrong when a knowledgeable and experienced coach fails to make a significant impact, despite providing top-notch coaching? The answer is usually due to one of two possibilities: Either the coachee is uncoachable or the style used by the coach is ineffective and inappropriate for the coachee. When asked about coaching effectiveness, many clients say that their coaches often do not coach them the way they want to be coached. Instead of reacting to that message as the "whine" of those who were resistant to change, we decided to look honestly at the issues surrounding coaching effectiveness and see if there was any foundation to these complaints. Drawing on research involving more than two thousand coaching clients in business organizations, we developed a research-based approach to coaching that yields effective results in nearly every engagement.

What goes wrong when a knowledgeable and experienced coach fails to make a significant impact, despite providing top-notch coaching? The answer is usually due to one of two possibilities: Either the coachee is uncoachable or the style used by the coach is ineffective and inappropriate for the coachee. When asked about coaching effectiveness, many clients say that their coaches often do not coach them the way they want to be coached. Instead of reacting to that message as the 'whine' of those who were resistant to change, we decided to look honestly at the issues surrounding coaching effectiveness and see if there was any foundation to these complaints. Drawing on research involving more than two thousand coaching clients in business organizations, we developed a research-based approach to coaching that yields effective results in nearly every engagement.

This research was prompted initially by the anecdotal reports we received from several individuals—many of whom were engaged with us in coaching interventions. We asked clients what their coaches should or could do to be more effective and the answers we received showed a complexity we were just beginning to understand. On the one hand, some clients told us that they would like their coaches to "be more to the point," "more specific and outspoken," and suggested a desire for what we call directive coaching. However, this represented only 39 percent of the research participants. Eighty-three percent said they preferred the coach to ask questions and help them explore the issues themselves, signaling a desire for a more nondirective form of coaching. In addition, some clients indicated that they preferred different types of coaching under different circumstances. Traditionally, most coaches had one style of coaching that they personally preferred and this was the approach they used with all of their clients. Without acknowledging the diversity and individual needs in the coaching relationship, it was little wonder that so many clients in the corporate world did not feel coaching was delivering on its promise. In coaching, we learned, one size does not fit all. Our research supports the intuitively obvious notion that when coaches modify their approach for each client, they achieve better results, higher levels of client satisfaction, and more measurable business results.

Between 1996 and 2002, Lore International Institute conducted an extensive survey of coaching effectiveness with Fortune 500 companies. The results of this study found that:

- Sixty-five percent of clients say that they want better coaching than they are getting
- Fifty-six percent of clients report that their coaching is often not focused on the right things
- Forty-five percent say the coaching they have received has not had much impact on their performance.

Based on these findings and years of professional coaching, we sought to develop an approach that will help ensure the effectiveness of coaching interventions and increase client satisfaction with coaching results.

In developing a matrix of coaching style preferences, our research confirmed that employing an *adaptive coaching* approach yields more effective results. How and when a coach gives help, and the focus of the coaching can make the difference between a successful intervention and one that does not satisfy the client and or have the desired impact.

We determined that another paradigm was required if coaching was to successfully impact the business world. However, many of the alternative models drew from the sports-coaching model. Notable sports figures as Vince Lombardi and Don Shula, who co-authored Everyone's a Coach, with Ken Blanchard, had a record of successes. However, their methods relied chiefly on one coaching model: the coach-as-leader, the coach who knows precisely what we need and whose criticism stings but motivates us to perform in ways we never thought ourselves capable. Blanchard and Shula (1995) wrote, "it's the coach's—the leader's beliefs that are most important; they become self-fulfilling." But our research led to a different end in the context of coaching the business professional. Many of our business coachees were, themselves, already in the position of 'the coach'. They were already the vision-making leaders and the tone-setters for their teams. While we enjoyed the sports anecdotes and found some of the principles transferable, we could see that athletic coaching and what our business-leader clients were telling us they needed, were often not the same. Our research indicated that a better model required involving the business leader as a responsible participant in the coaching process.

Over the years, Lore has always embraced an experiential approach to effective adult learning. Much of the pioneering research in this area came from the seminal work of Carl Rogers (1961) who challenged traditional psychoanalytic approaches by arguing that therapists should allow patients to discover the solution for themselves. In effect, Rogers made the client at least equally responsible for finding a solution, rejecting the authoritative analytical approaches used by psychotherapists, experimental, or even behavioral therapists. Rogers evolved a set of steps in the learning and growth process that might be summarized as:

1. **The individual comes for help.**
   This is the most significant step within the steps of therapy. The individual has taken it upon himself to take the first step for help even if he does not recognize this as the reason he's there.

2. **The helping situation is defined.**
   The client is made aware that the counselor does not have the answers, but that with assistance he can, work out his own solutions to his problems.

3. **The counselor encourages free expression of feelings in regard to the problem.**
   The counselor provides the client with a friendly, interested, and receptive attitude, which helps to bring about free expression.

4. **The counselor accepts, recognizes, and clarifies negative feelings.**
   Whatever the negative feelings are the counselor must say and do things, which helps the client recognize the negative feelings at hand.

5. **When the individual's negative feelings have been expressed they are followed by expressions of positive impulses which make for growth.**

6. **The counselor accepts and recognizes the positive feelings in the same manner as the negative feelings.**

7. **There is insight, understanding of the self, and acceptance of the self along with possible courses of actions.**
   This is the next important aspect because it allows for new levels.

8. **Then comes the step of positive action along with the decreasing the need for help** (Rogers, 1951).

This client-centered approach has proven especially effective in adult learning theory, as it places the adult learner at the center of the developmental equation.

Critics of Rogers have pointed out that idealizing a fully functioning personality as one that is self-actualizing and very open to experience depends heavily on the receptiveness of the individual subject. These critics note that Rogers was infused with a kind of unreflective optimism about the "intuitive sense of human freedom"(Maddi, 1996). A number of Rogers' critics point out that there is little empirical evidence for his belief in an 'innate' drive to self-actualize (Krebs and Blackman, 1988; Maddi, 1996). Further, Rogers' notion of personality extremes—namely his concepts of an Ideal Self as opposed to a Maladjusted Self—is really an oversimplification. His idea was that incongruencies between the self and experience are the fundamental sources of maladjustment. His faith in the rationality of humans, and their ability to consciously bring their experiences into alignment with their idea of a perfected 'self' can seem overly naïve.

From the clinical psychologist's point of view, we can understand these criticisms. But when applying Rogers' ideas to the problems of executives, they are less problematic. For one thing, high-performing adults who operate within the general range of human normalcy are not looking to resolve the deep and core personality issues that drive clinical psychology. Rogers' ideas make more sense when they are applied to a person-centered approach to enhancing performance, particularly for persons who are already well on the way to being fully self-actualized. If one looks at Rogers' notions as being an extension of a human science instead of a natural or a social science, they have solid value for the business coaching profession.

Still, applying Rogers' models to coaching, which had so long been allied to certain kinds of therapy, was not as intuitive as it might appear. Business coaching, and the performance metrics required in corporations, did not readily lend themselves to this type of self-realization model. Left without some sort of tangible way to measure the results, the Rogerian approach—even with its benefits—could readily fall back into the sort of self-help programs that had produced the negative feedback found in our own and other studies of coaching.

Rogers provided a baseline for the creation of our model, but in a business context, we needed also to define a process that could provide a real metric of results. Such metrics for coaching are sometimes challenging to obtain and a good many coaching enterprises urge caution when seeking to measure the effectiveness of coaching. Yet this was exactly what so many clients and coaching customers wanted.

There are many possible models, but the one our research found to be most relevant was Kirkpatrick's Model of Evaluation. Kirkpatrick's (1998) four level model was one with which many in the training industry were already familiar but its evaluation criteria make it an excellent tool for the coaching environment as well. For example, the first of the four levels of evaluation is the participant's reaction to the training, sometimes referred to as a "smile sheet." To apply this technique to coaching would entail little more than determining how the executives responded to the coaching. What did they like or dislike about the coaching process and the coach? Level Two assesses the learning that has taken place. What did the executive learn during the coaching process? What evidence do we have that the executive acquired new skills, developed new attitudes or perspectives, and learned new things? Level Three assesses how learning is transferred from the learning scenario to the job. Finally, Level Four measures business results. How has the coaching led to improvements in business performance?

The move to coaching from other forms of training has been largely led by organizations that were frustrated with the results of mere training alone. Our own study (Bacon and Spear, 2003) as well as others (e.g., Michaels, 2001) showed that the move to coaching had come because traditional classroom training was not leading to sustained behavioral changes and to long-term learning transfer.

In an earlier and more heady coaching climate, the coaching literature had made eloquent claims about personal growth, unleashed human potential, and enhanced creativity. These grandiose claims soured in the ears of our business coaching clients. We set monumental expectations and the business world naturally grew skeptical.

The Kirkpatrick model for measuring coaching provided a kind of stable link to experience, validated in nearly 30 years of measuring training programs. This meant that adapting Kirkpatrick as a beginning point for measuring coaching effectiveness, and coupling that system with a Rogerian-style approach to coaching interventions, would allow us to postulate a model that both addressed the issues uncovered in our research and also provided a means for testing this model against a well-validated baseline.

We were not looking to create a panacea. Instead the model we were creating was being driven by factors in the research and rooted in our own experiences in coaching practice. Early on, we had provided coaching in much the same way as many others: we sought to connect with a coachee; identify key issues; suggest some workable solutions; provide encouraging advice; and hope for the best. In our twenty years of coaching, however, we learned that this approach seldom achieved effective results in the business environment.

To compound this issue, most of us get our base life coaching from parents, teachers, athletic coaches, spiritual advisors, or other kinds of authority figures. These well-intentioned people tend to coach and teach us in a fairly directive manner—in other words they tend to "tell us what to do. In the early stages of our learning, this kind of directive approach works well. We know little, have little experience, and have a limited frame of reference. When a parent, teacher, or authority figure says, "Do this," we tend to fall in line. That pattern gets reinforced when the outcomes of that sort of directive approach get favorable results. Most of us, then, get conditioned to look for an expert (authority figure) who will simply tell us what to do.

But when the corporate executive reaches the level of being that authority figure, to whom do they turn? Often, they follow this directive pattern by hiring an outside "expert" who takes that very authoritarian stance. Unfortunately, in the complicated world of business, that approach no longer consistently yields the easy results. The realities of corporate business are simply too messy to allow a simplistic handle-it-this-way kind of thinking. There are, of course, those instances when a directive approach is the most appropriate course. For example, you wouldn't want an expert coach to be teaching you how to operate a piece of heavy equipment and ask, "How do you think this equipment works?" Directive coaching is appropriate when you are imparting knowledge, explaining how to do something or showing a client how something works, or when you don't have time to do anything more. Obviously, directive coaching is also the right approach when a client asks for advice and when it is what the client wants.

So for the top company leaders, the need is not for a coach who provides answers, but for a Rogerian-type counselor who will ask good questions and elicit self-revelatory responses from the coachee. To balance the directive approach predicted by our backgrounds, we came to call this evolution of Rogerian techniques non-directive coaching. In our minds, these two categories co-exist in any effective coaching arrangement. As we have noted, some circumstances lend themselves well to giving direction. But for executives in leading roles, far more prefer a non-directive approach. Non-directive coaching appeals to people's need for self-sufficiency and self-directed growth and calls for the coach to rely on two primary skills: asking and listening in a way that helps the coachee work through issues and arrive at the right conclusions for themselves.

How does a coach determine the right response? As the Rogerian model suggests, the only way is to adapt on a case-by-case basis. We came to see that an ideologically sound approach to effective coaching can only happen when the coach adapts to the needs of the coachee. Hence we labeled our model *Adaptive Coaching.*

You might suppose with this distinction we had arrived. But on the face of it, simply adapting in a directive or a non-directive manner won't result in an effective coaching intervention. We knew this because, once again, our research was telling us that many coaches had already intuitively adopted this approach. However, many of the problems faced by executives either required immediate solutions—they were circumstantial—or they stemmed from broad issues that were systemic to their corporate environments—in other words, they were programmatic. Our objective in this had always been to find a means of modeling the key elements of our adaptive coaching approach into a useable and repeatable process that coaches could readily apply and that would optimize results against the identified issues our research had uncovered.

This understanding resulted in a preliminary model that formed a crude matrix. A base model of this type could initially enable a coach to begin working with an executive and ask the kinds of Rogerian questions that would identify the real, underlying issues in terms of the categories we had thus far identified. Still, this model seemed very thin.

Many executives told us that often their needs were of a very specific nature. Some of the early coaching approaches had tended to ignore this in favor of more clinical models that sought to address the needs of the whole person. Our research simply underscored that in business many of the core issues and needs center on highly specific needs. Sweeping interventions that asked coachees to address larger scale issues like work/life balance, quality of life, or even Rogerian-style self-awareness did not address the need.

It was at this juncture that we modified and altered our Rogerian approach. Experience working directly with the executive in the trenches demonstrated that there were times when the correct coaching adaptation was to focus specifically and directively on a fixed circumstance. To reflect this we modified the model to incorporate additional levels of complexity. The result was a matrix that still had a number of holes.

Looking at the revised matrix, it seemed obvious to us that if circumstances could be specific, they might also be systemic or holistic. To test this we again referenced our research and saw that of the 56% we found who said coaching was "not focused on the right thing" (Bacon and Spear, 2003), many noted coaching's failure to effectively address systemic or holistic problems that were of a circumstantial nature. This meant for our model to work well, we had to add a holistic category:

Many coaches in the field because of their own larger interests in the more program-matic or visionary aspects of coaching centering on quality of life issues, transformation, and even spiritual renewal issues. Our survey found that coaches who did not ask the right kinds of Rogerian-style questions, designed to learn what an executive was really seeking to resolve, could miss or ignore key circumstantial problems that were the client's entire reason for engaging a coach.

That said, didn't the research confirm that the more visionary aspects of coaching—

what we were modeling as programmatic—could still be a major focus of the executive coaching process? The answer was, of course, yes. Many of our coaching survey respondents were seeking that broader vision through coaching. Looked at in one way, such a quest might nullify the directive elements of coaching at the programmatic level. Many—including many of my Lore colleagues and me—engage in coaching because they are interested in the more open-ended aspects of personality, vision, and leadership. Those qualities would seem to eliminate both the directive and specific elements of the model we were evolving.

But again we retuned to our research and our hands-on coaching experiences. Sixty percent of our survey respondents said that they wanted better coaching than they were getting (Bacon and Spear, 2003). We wondered what that meant. The survey pointed to the answer: 56% said that coaching was not helping them learn exactly what they should do differently to be more effective (Bacon and Spear, 2003). The term "exactly" confirmed that many executives still wanted some directive coaching—even when the reasons for coaching were more programmatic and vision-shaping. Thus, a fully adaptive coaching model required keeping both a directive and a specific form of coaching as an option in the model, and in coaching practice. The result was now to have an adaptive coaching model that was increasingly complex because it reflected the actual complexities and hierarchies of needs required by executives for coaching to achieve measurable business results:

	DIRECTIVE		NONDIRECTIVE	
	SPECIFIC	HOLISTIC	SPECIFIC	HOLISTIC
PROGRAMMATIC	Teacher	Parent	Facilitator	Counselor
CIRCUMSTANTIAL	Manager	Philosopher	Colleague	Mentor

As a broadband tool of categories, we could look at this matrix and see that it covered a fairly large range and scope of possible coaching approaches. The Rogerian method suggests that all of these are actually continuums, where a Non-Directive, Specific, Programmatic coaching intervention could flow into a Non-Directive, Holistic, Programmatic intervention. The matrix we evolved, therefore, is not a rigid set of prescribed categories. It is indeed a model, intended for use by coaching professionals as a guideline to adapting their coaching styles to the needs and preferences of individual coachees. Based on our research and experience, we can confirm that taking this kind of adaptive approach almost always results in meaningful and measurably effective coaching interventions with business executives.

To clarify the model and make it more useful, we added some sample coaching personae to each quadrant. The idea of these sample personae is to allow the coach to frame and benchmark the style of coaching that generally fits that category. Our Adaptive Coaching Model as it has currently evolved is as follows:

	Directive Approach		**Non-Directive Approach**	
	Specific	Holistic	Specific	Holistic
Circumstantial				
	Specific	Holistic	Specific	Holistic
Programmatic				

As our research and work on this model continue, we are looking at incorporating the continuums between all of the elements of this matrix to allow for even greater refinements in the adaptability of the model and the coaching styles that we can now link to it.

Using Kirkpatrick's Four Levels of Assessment—and employing validated assessment instruments against this adaptive model—demonstrates that this approach yields measurable results in the following areas shown in Figure 3:

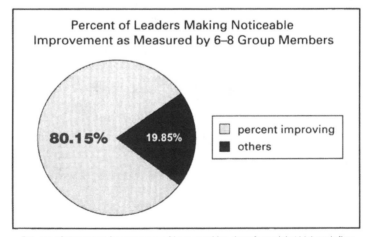

*source of data taken from surveys of Lore coaching done for a global high-tech firm

Figure 3

To check our use of the Kirkpatrick model to measure results in terms of our adaptive coaching approach, we collaborated with a key client, a leading technology firm, to do an ROI study of our coaching for their firm. In very simple terms, ROI can be calculated as: ROI = (Benefits – Costs/Costs) x 100

This leading technology firm had initially engaged with us to coach only its most senior executives. In the beginning, the firm advanced cautiously because they wanted and required results-based accountability. As the first coaching interventions proceeded, we were able to document success in terms of Kirkpatrick's scale, but the numbers of engagements were still small and, therefore, statistically suspect. However, the Kirkpatrick Level 1 responses from the coached executives were so favorable that we initiated a process to cascade coaching to additional levels within the firm.

After a number of months, we had engaged with more than 60 senior executives and leaders within this worldwide company, so we now had a sample population that could have statistical validity. Accordingly, we co-developed a survey instrument designed to collect responses from individuals inside the firm who would be able to respond against the four levels defined in the Kirkpatrick model. These included the Level 1 responders (self-satisfaction); the Level 2 responders (self-learnings); the Level 3 responders (transfer by observable changes noted by others); and the Level 4 responders (business results monitors). The surveys were sent specifically for each individual coachee and responses were collected from throughout the organization. The results of this data collection are reflected in this graphic:

Lore's Coaching Tools for Measuring Impact

For data validity reasons, we required a minimum of six responders at all of Kirkpatrick's four levels. The number of coachees that were deemed to have made noticeable improvement was actually just over the 80th percentile. This is a significant shift from the 45% we quoted at the opening of this paper who said coaching did not have much of an impact. To go from nearly half of coachees saying coaching was ineffective to over 80% indicating that our approach produced tangible ROI indicates that the Adaptive Coaching Model works.

Carl Rogers said, "In my early professional years I was asking the question: How can I treat, or cure, or change this person? Now I would phrase the question in this way: How can I provide a relationship which this person may use for his own personal growth?" The coach's work is helping people grow, achieve, or overcome. Adapting to the needs and preferences of their clients requires that coaches establish in the beginning of the relationship and throughout what clients need. Coaches who ignore clients' preferences in favor of their own are usually less effective in the long run because they aren't uncovering and acknowledging what the client really needs and how he prefers to acquire it. By adhering to an adaptive coaching model, coaches can increase their impact in measurable ways while adhering to the loftier goal of helping people grow.

References

Bacon, T. R. & Spear, K. (2003). *Adaptive coaching: The art and practice of a client-centered approach to performance improvement.* Palto Alto, CA: Davies-Black Publishing.

Blanchard, K. & Shula, D. (1995). *Everyone's a coach.* Grand Rapids, MI: Zondervan Publishing.

Darwin, C. (1979). *The origin of species.* New York, NY: Random House.

Kirkpatrick, D. (1998). Evaluating training programs. New York, NY: Berrett-Koehler Publishers.

Krebs, D. & Blackman, R. (1988). *Psychology: A first encounter.* New York, NY: Hartcourt College Publishing.

Maddi, S. (1996). *Personality theories: A comparative analysis.* Prospective Heights, IL: Waveland Press.

Michaels, E., Handfield-Jones, H., & Axelrod, B. (2001). *The war for talent.* Cambridge, MA: Harvard University Press.

Rogers, C. (1951). *Client centered therapy.* New York, NY: Houghton Mifflin.

Rogers, C. (1961). *On becoming a person.* New York, NY: Houghton Mifflin.

Ryckmann, R. M. (1993). *Theories of personality.* Los Angeles, CA: Brooks/Cole Publishing Co.

Terry Bacon, Ph.D. is President and CEO of Lore International Institute. He has more than 25 years of experience in leadership development, coaching, executive education, and client relationship management. He is author of numerous books, research reports, and white papers. He is the author or coauthor of a number of assessments, including the Coaching Effectiveness Survey, the Lore Leadership Assessment, and, most recently, the Leadership Balance Sheet™. Dr. Bacon earned his B.S. in engineering from the United States Military Academy at West Point and a Ph.D. from The American University. He has also studied at Roosevelt University; Goddard College; the University of Chicago; Stanford University; the Wharton School of Business; and, the Harvard Business School. Contact: bacon@lorenet.com

Building Dialogue for Effective Change: Coaching with the Five Principles of Appreciative Inquiry

Sara Orem
Ann Clancy
Jacqueline Binkert

This paper defines the five principles underlying the philosophy of Appreciative Inquiry (AI) and demonstrates how the conscious use of these five principles may enable more joyful, interactive, and effective coaching relationships than those methodologies based on a problem-solving approach. The paper grounds coaching in AI's theoretical framework. Samples from three case studies describe how these principles more effectively engage the client with the coach, provide more focus to the client's own goal setting, and move to enthusiastic action in the change process.

The quality of the dialogue between coach and client, and the client's actions taken, readily demonstrate the significance of these principles to coaching. A second significant difference between coaching using Appreciative principles and that which uses problem-solving, is the extended positive attitude of both the coach and the client toward self, history, action and goals over the entire period of the coaching relationship.

The development and implementation of a coaching design based on the principles and philosophy of Appreciative Inquiry demonstrate in practice the propositions embedded in the principles. More simply put, the practice of AI in one-to-one coaching relationships supports the notion, originally posed by Lewin (in Schein) that there is nothing so practical as a good theory. The use of these five principles produces both a more positive and a more effective dialogue in the pursuit of change.

Introduction

Appreciative Inquiry (AI) developed over twenty years ago at Case Western Reserve University through the action research of a group of graduate students who found problem solving to be an over-used method for effecting change in organizations (Cooperrider and Srivastva, 1987). The original research used AI to elicit stories of past successes at a major regional hospital as a framework for thinking about change as an extension of competencies, strengths and skills already possessed by individuals and the organization. While Appreciative Inquiry has been of benefit to a number of other positive methods for change, in positive psychology (Seligman, 2002), sociology (Keyes and Haidt, 2003), and organizational effectiveness (positive organizational scholarship, Cameron, Dutton, and Quinn, 2003), it has found its usefulness primarily in and with groups.

The change design of Appreciative Inquiry is fairly simple. A topic arises out of current concerns about change. A group or team charged with designing a change process first Discovers (Cooperrider and Srivastva, 1987) about their past successes in the area of change they've chosen to investigate. Where have they shown they could excel before?

How did that feel to be so successful, and what were the results of their past successes? Once these stories of discovery are collected, the same group, or a larger one (AI seeks to engage the largest possible representation of the organization) Dreams about what these evident successes might mean for a future organization, and how these successes might be applied to create the desired change. Next, the organization Designs the future, using past successes as a leverage point for action in the direction of change. Finally, the organization finds its Destiny in the desired future and seeks to embed the change in all parts of the organization.

As organization consultants and coaches, it struck us that the same philosophy might profitably be applied to one-to-one coaching relationships. Briefly, the topic choice relates easily to goal identification. The Discover stage builds a framework for the coach's knowing of the client's past successes and what abilities and preferences might be leveraged toward the desired goal. At the same time coaches and clients build trust as they get to know each other. The Dream stage relates easily to goal setting, that is, how can the client use her past successes to build a dream of the future? The Design stage relates to the ongoing dance between the coach and client of defining action steps and experimenting with them. Finally, Destiny relates to a culmination of the relationship, or the summation of a goal achieved and redefinition of another (perhaps broader) goal.

Where an Appreciative Inquiry modeled change process may differ from traditional goal setting and achievement is in the focus. AI does not see change as a problem to be solved, but as a dream to be realized. Client's shortcomings or weaknesses are only indirectly addressed, whereas their strengths are emphasized and consciously applied. To the degree that many coaching methods emphasize the positive, AI is similar. To the degree that other methods concentrate on solutions (to problems), it is different.

In addition to the four stages of Appreciative Inquiry, five principles underlie its philosophy (Ricketts and Willis, 2001). It is these principles that inform the case studies in this paper.

Principle 1: The Constructionist Principle

This principle posits that knowing and destiny are interwoven. Postmodern scholars believe that empirical truths are few, so that there are, in reality, not very many generalizations we can make, or sure predictors of repeatable interactions. However, who we are and how we became who we are is a strong predictor (not fate, mind you) of who we can and will become. In other words, our future is an extension of what we know and don't know, both as coach and client. Our actions (what we are doing and have done) contribute to our current reality, and put boundaries around what we believe we can be. By inquiring about a client's past success, we determine what the client knows, and how we can apply what he knows to a desirable future.

Principle 2: The Principle of Simultaneity

Inquiry and change happen simultaneously, according to this principle. The seeds of change are sown by the very first questions we ask. They create the foundations for what we discover, and our discoveries become the foundations for dreaming and designing our destinies. Often this is slow, and sometimes painful, as we shall see from the case studies.

However, our insistence on framing stories positively eventually engages the client in her own dream.

Principle 3: The Poetic Principle

The poetic principle suggests that an individual's story can be rewritten any time. Any number of new realities can flow from a reinterpretation of one's life story, just as there are any number of potential interpretations of a poem. Not all coaching clients come with positive life stories. The Poetic Principle reminds the coach and the client that a story can be reframed, reimagined, and refocused to enable more hopeful and joyful action toward a desired change.

Principle 4: The Anticipatory Principle

This principle states that a particular vision of the future can guide current behavior in the direction of that future; that is, the anticipation of a particular future will naturally lead to certain actions in the present. To this end, an Appreciative Coaching approach focuses clients on a positive vision to enable them to take clearer action in the present toward that vision. For some clients, it can be frightening to clearly define a desired future, especially if they are accustomed to living a negative life story. In such cases, it may be that not identifying or not taking action has actually contributed to moving them away from the future they want.

Principle 5: The Positive Principle

Positive attitudes, actions and connections influence long-term change. The more positive all of these components remain, the longer-lasting the change. This is an overarching principle for our appreciative coaching practice. It suggests that when both the coach and the client are connected as partners in the positive pursuit of a goal, and when they both retain (mostly) positive attitudes and act toward the change they want, the change will happen. It may happen more quickly than through traditional problem solving as clients-even very negative ones- change so that they can perceive themselves as effective actors in their own behalf.

The Three Case Studies

As three coaches/authors, we formed eight coaching relationships each lasting over nine sessions and approximately five months in 2004-2005. Protocols included (a) beginning with a Client Information form asking potential participants to fill out a five page positive history (thereby beginning the Discovery stage), (b)focus in the sessions on positive questions and client experimentation (Dreaming and Designing), and (c)ongoing written reflections by the coaches. These reflections examined our own use of positive questions and language in general, and whether that attempt to stay in the positive had an influence on the language and action of the client. It is in the coaches' self-reflections that the clearest indicators of the Principles can be found. Three of these relationships will be described in some detail to illustrate the use of the Five Principles of Appreciative Inquiry. The names of both the coaches and the clients have been changed to protect the clients' confidentiality.

Susan was without a job and without much hope when she began her coaching relationship with Helen. Her goal was to get a job she wanted and liked, unlike the job she had left. She "viewed herself as her limitations and she acknowledged that she did this." She responded to positive questions with negative and self-deprecating answers. While she readily agreed to keep a journal, for instance, her content consisted of such statements as, "I didn't rescue anyone from a fire." Susan's perception of her current reality seemed to be based on her past actions (or inactions). She "bracketed" what she believed about her lack of past successes and applied this belief to the future, demonstrating the Constructionist Principle both in her view of her life, and in her inaction.

It took great energy for Helen to stay with Susan in a positive frame. Susan seemed to need layer upon layer of positive reinforcement in order to begin to see herself as worth her own attention. Helen reported her client's negative framing influenced her as a coach and she experienced some low energy, occasional depression (matching her client's), and headaches. But Helen stuck with the appreciative approach. The seeds of change were germinating, but they weren't yet visible. Four months into the relationship, Helen posed the question as to whether she was the right coach for Susan. Perhaps, Helen wondered aloud, Susan could better work with a career coach. Susan surprised Helen with her response. She said that she didn't think she needed that expertise, and that she saw Helen's role as helping her to define everything. According to Helen, "She (Susan) was very positive about her role in the relationship and during the rest of our session, she was very active." Susan began here to demonstrate the Poetic Principle of reinterpreting her own life story, and beginning to be able to construct new realities as a result. She began to take a more active role in finding a job for herself, and when the first job fell through, she was able to bounce back with some equanimity. Given the disappointment, Helen was "surprised to find her in pretty good spirits for our call. She had gotten past the anger and was looking to take action." "She is definitely identifying and agreeing to taking on more action steps for the coming week. She's also willing to stretch, to try something out." Susan had begun to identify a particular vision of the future, one with a full-time job, and she was guiding her own behavior in the direction of that vision, a clear demonstration of the Anticipatory Principle.

Susan got a new job. It wasn't a perfect job. In their last call she could, however, see the positive aspects of it for herself (as well as the negative). Helen affirmed that Susan was in a better position now to seek the job she really wanted, rather than any job for the sake of a paycheck. Her movement from pervasively negative to occasionally or often positive was an indication of the presence of the Positive Principle. Although this was a most difficult relationship for Helen, it represented movement in the direction of positive attitudes, actions and connections for Susan.

Carlos, in contrast to Susan, was seemingly the ideal client for an Appreciative coaching approach, or perhaps any coaching approach. He was "intense, motivated and clear about what he wanted." Throughout the nine sessions Carlos used mostly positive language, and his coach Casey's positive approach questions, "elicited a clear identification of action steps for what he wants more of." Both Carlos and Casey easily demonstrated the overarching positive principle. When Carlos was tentative about his ability to get something he wanted (to be president of a professional association), Casey helped him to reframe his desire by using both the Constructionist Principle (seeing past success to predict future successes), and the Poetic Principle (reframing his view of his own capabilities) to move him to action toward his vision. Casey affirms this in their next session when she reports that he is "very quick to incorporate suggestions and changes in reframing the way he looks at things."

When Carlos articulated something difficult he wanted to address in approaching a senior manager, Casey was able to help him think of steps he might take as "experiments" to guide his current behavior toward his desired goal, demonstrations of the Anticipatory Principle.

In succeeding sessions Carlos became increasingly aware of Casey's drawing him into a positive frame for his action steps, particularly in her use of "What?" questions—i.e., "What will you do to make sure that this is a productive meeting?" At the end of their sessions, Carlos told Casey that he had been "the most proactive he'd been in a long time" citing his own ability now to use "what" questions. This demonstrates the presence of the Principle of Simultaneity as Casey's questions, and then Carlos', became the foundations for Dreaming and Designing his future.

Madeleine came to Alex having been a high achieving marketing executive for many years. She was facing her first sustained period of dissatisfaction with her organization and her role in that organization. Although she reported being a generally optimistic and upbeat person, her affect was somewhat "flat" in the first few sessions, and she eventually sought medical help for what she saw as her own worrisome behavior. From the outset, Alex reframed her professional situation as not so much about Madeleine as about the change in the organizational environment, reflecting changed expectations of Madeleine's role. As Madeleine began to reframe what she had previously seen as personal attacks, she looked at her changed role with more neutral eyes. She looked forward to experimenting with "seeing possibilities" rather than "thinking in circles," a demonstration of the Poetic Principle.

As Madeleine prepared for her review, Alex encouraged her to think of her "best outcomes" within the current organization framework. Madeleine reviewed her own performance and formulated questions of the President about his expectations for her and the firm in the coming year, to "get and share information." She ultimately reframed the review as "a learning experience." The actual review met her positive expectations and more; she got a bonus she was not expecting.

After a holiday vacation Madeleine returned to work to find that her firm was in a frenzy of preparation for presentation to a new client (actually an old client returning because of Madeleine). Various moves on the part of the founder and President set Madeleine back a few steps. However, because she had begun to live in a more positive frame, she determined that her own value could not be dictated by these negative interactions. Currently, Madeleine is examining her considerable strengths to find areas where she can profitably engage them for her own increased well-being. She demonstrates the Constructionist Principle by mindfully applying her strengths in the present so that she will be prepared for a professional opportunity that best fits her style, needs and gifts.

Discussion

The stages of Appreciative Inquiry easily can be understood in a coaching framework, but they do depart from the usual definition of a problem/solution approach that includes setting a goal, exploring the current situation for clues as to possible supports and barriers to achievement of the goal, brainstorming possible actions, and then committing to certain actions (Whitmore's GROW model, 2002). The AI approach seeks to Discover past successes that can be leveraged toward the desired goal, builds a Dream for the future using past successes, begins to Design current action steps through experimentation, and finally, supports the client in achieving her goal or Destiny through the use of the five principles of Appreciative Inquiry.

The approach is not easy, however. For the three coaches in this study, the pull toward negativity (at times sustained), on the part of some clients, was frequent. To stay within a framework of past success, current achievement, and future possibilities is harder than one might think. Our organizational structures are overwhelmingly predicated on problem solving, and many clients are used to seeking a helping professional to solve a problem or fix a weakness. It takes concerted effort to model a different perspective, one that sometimes gives headaches, or at least self-questioning.

The AI framework positions the client clearly as the expert and removes the ego satisfaction of having the "right" answers for the coach. While all coaching has client expertise as a guidepost, it is often tempting to share our considerable experience with a floundering client. With AI, the coach can't know a client's past successes, her current strengths, or what is really right for her future— only the client can say what her positive future will be.

Finally, while the stages provide the framework, the principles provide the foundation for the coach to stay in a positive frame, to encourage the client to rewrite interpretations, and to rethink what is possible.

Implications and Lessons Learned

As coaches, each of us uses an array of coaching methodologies with our clients. For the purpose of this study, we focused on an Appreciative Inquiry approach to test our assumptions about applying the five principles to the coaching relationship. Appreciative Inquiry is a significant philosophy and one that informs every action and conversation we have with clients. We are not suggesting that it "cures" everything. Helen's client will still seek more suitable employment. Casey's client may find that he has deeper needs he wishes to explore. Madeleine, Alex's client, remains in a powerfully negative environment for reasons that make sense now.

We believe that the Appreciative Inquiry approach does engage clients in a powerfully different way from problem-solving. Overall, our experience was that positive questions encouraged positive responses. Focusing on current strengths and past successes, clients began to reframe possibilities on their own. We found that action steps framed as experiments gave clients permission to try things they might have avoided due to fear of failure.

To make sure our perceptions as coaches are more than self-fulfilling prophesies (a possible criticism of our first phase of research), we have embarked on a second phase. The stories in this paper are drawn from our first research phase in which we have described only our own observations and reflections as coaches and quoted from our clients' evaluations. In Phase II of our research study, we further test our assumptions by taping sessions with three more clients (one per coach for a total of 9 sessions each). The transcripts from these sessions will be coded and independently assessed for evidence of five main foci:

1. Evidence of the application of the five AI principles in the coaching process
2. Use by the coach of client's existing successes and strengths in co-designing a desired future
3. Positive questioning by the coach and positive responses from the client
4. The client's willingness to experiment and enthusiasm for experimenting
5. Ultimate results (living into a desired future).

In addition, we will continue to record our reflections after each session. We will present the results of both phases of our research.

Summary

Many effective coaching methods exist in addition to Appreciative Inquiry Coaching. Like other coaches, we explore and apply a variety of approaches that we deem most helpful to our clients. While we are not suggesting that Appreciative Inquiry is the best coaching method to replace others, we are finding that it provides an encouraging and hopeful path that some clients may find uniquely helpful in designing and accomplishing personal and professional change.

The importance of this research for coaching is that the Appreciative approach, and particularly its five guiding principles, enable positive self-perception in those clients used to defining themselves by things they need to fix, and enhance the ability to leverage strengths for those who already see themselves as strong and effective. For the coach, the methodology encourages self-reflection about the coach's own strengths and abilities and magnifies where coaching is most effective.

References

Cameron, K. S., Dutton, J. E., & Quinn, R. E. (2003). *Positive organizational scholarship: Foundations of a new discipline.* San Francisco, CA: Berrett-Koehler.

Cooperrider, D. & Srivastva, S. (1987). Appreciative Inquiry. In R. W. Woodman & W.A. Pasmore (eds.) *Research in organizational change and development. Vol. 1* (pp. 129-169). New York: JAI Press.

Keyes, C.L. & Haidt, J. (Eds.) (2003). *Flourishing: Positive psychology and the life well-lived.* Washington, DC: American Psychological Association.

Ricketts, M. W., & Willis, J. E. (2001). *Experiencing AI: A practitioner's guide to integrating appreciative inquiry with experiential learning.* Taos, NM: The Taos Institute.

Schein, E. H. Kurt Lewin's change theory in the field and in the classroom: Notes toward a model of managed learning. Retreived 4/3/05 from http://www.a2zpsychology.com/ARTICLES/kurt_lewin's_change_theory.htm

Seligman, M. E. P. (2002). *Authentic happiness.* New York: Free Press.

Whitmore, J. (2002). *Coaching for performance: GROWing people, performance and purpose.* London: Nicholas Brealey.

Sara Orem, Ph.D. has twenty years of management experience and fifteen years management consulting in and to major financial services companies in the U. S., Britain and Australia. While most of her career has been spent in banks, insurance companies and brokerage firms, she has a strong affiliation, and has had multiple consulting relationships, with major non-profits. In her corporate and non-profit work Dr. Orem has consulted to a full-spectrum of organizational roles from operations to boards of directors. In addition to coaching, Sara teaches both an advanced coaching course for managers and a team development course for Capella University. She is qualified to interpret, has presented workshops, and published papers about the Myers Briggs Type Indicator and is co-author of Living Simply. She earned a doctorate degree in Human and Organization Systems at Fielding University where her dissertation was focused on transformative learning in interpersonal conflict. Her current focus is on positive methods including Appreciative Inquiry in coaching and group processes. Contact: slocookin@comcast.net.

Ann Clancy, Ph.D., is a business coach and an executive consultant, professional facilitator with expertise in cultural diversity and community planning, and a researcher in qualitative studies. As an organization development professional, she incorporates the appreciative Inquiry approach into her strategic planning with a wide range of clients-from community groups and non-profit organizations to corporations and governmental agencies. She coaches executives, small business owners, professionals and teams in strategic and performance related issues. She earned a doctorate in Organization Development from the Fielding Graduate University. Contact: aclancy@clancyconsultants.net

Jacqueline Binkert, Ph.D., is an executive coach and organization development consultant who is experienced in working with leaders and their teams during times of major change and cultural transformation. She began her career as an adult educator working with multi-lingual and multi-cultural adults of wide-ranging capabilities and backgrounds. She then moved to the business world where, as an internal consultant for Ford Motor Company, she acquired expertise in large-scale change in such areas as leading in a matrix, managing dispersed international teams, moving from functional to system responsibilities and adopting brand management. She now works independently, and her practice includes coaching executives in strategic leadership, leadership development and culture change. She is researching the application of Appreciative Inquiry to coaching. Her doctorate is in Human and Organizational Systems from the Fielding Graduate University. Contact: jbinkert@oeiconsulting.com.

Personal Coaching From the Client's Perspective

Valerie Erika Creane

This exploratory study provides a rich description of the nature and impact of coaching from the perspective of personal coaching clients. Qualitative methods were used to address the guiding research question: What is personal coaching from the perspective of the client? In-depth interviews were conducted with eight adults who were currently engaged in long-term coaching relationships with experienced coaches certified by the Coaches Training Institute. Inductive analysis was used to analyze the data, and member checks were conducted to verify the accuracy of data reduction.

Thirteen major themes were identified that address the nature and impact of personal coaching. Eight themes described the process of coaching: (a) identifies what clients want, (b) shifts clients' perspectives, (c) connects the client and coach in a powerful relationship, (d) promotes self-discovery, (e) focuses on the present and future rather than the past, (f) promotes client accountability, (g) identifies and challenges clients' internal barriers to success, and (h) follows the client's agenda. Three themes addressed the skills a coach utilizes during coaching: (a) listening, (b) asking thought-provoking questions, and (c) providing validation or acknowledgment. Four themes described the impact of coaching on clients: (a) becoming more aware of what they want, (b) self-discovery, (c) moving forward in their lives, and (d) feeling more positively about themselves.

The participants in the present study clearly articulated that coaching involves and results in goal identification, accountability, learning, action, and increased effectiveness– all factors discussed in the limited coaching literature. They also, however, described coaching as a ìsoulful,î heart-opening process that helped them connect with their deepest desires, their greatest strengths, and their overall life purposes. These results indicate that coaching provides a unique and distinctive helping relationship that bridges the worlds of psychological transformation and goal-oriented consulting.

Introduction

Coaches working with individuals in and outside of organizations often hear the question: "What is coaching?" This is a difficult question to answer, in part because coaching is an emerging profession that is only beginning to find a language to describe itself. To define coaching, and increase the credibility of coaching as a profession, empirical research must be conducted to determine the unique nature and impact of coaching.

Coaches, psychologists, consultants, human resource professionals, and journalists have raised concerns about the lack of empirical research on coaching (Brotman, Liberi, and Wasylyshyn, 1998; Creane, 2002; Garman, Whiston and Zlatoper, 2000; Kilburg, 1996b; Wilkins, 2000). While executive coaching, as one type of coaching, boasts a small body of conceptual and theoretical documentation, relatively little has been published about personal coaching. Much of the published material on personal coaching describes models of coaching written by coaches, or offers self-help coaching techniques to potential coaching clients.

In particular, little is known about how personal coaching clients experience coaching. Wilkins' (2000) study of coaching, which developed a grounded theory of coaching based on interviews with experienced personal coaches, provided important information about how coaches conceptualize coaching. Sztucinski's (2001) phenomenological investigation of executive coaching provided information about how executive clients experience the coaching process. The present study builds on these efforts by examining the practice of coaching from the perspective of the personal coaching client.

How do personal coaching clients experience coaching? What impact does coaching have on their lives? Learning more about how clients experience coaching will increase the understanding of what coaching is and how it differs from other helping relationships (such as therapy and consulting). This is essential, if coaches want to establish coaching as a valued profession that offers a distinct and unique service to clients with particular needs.

The present study used the experiences of personal coaching clients to explore the nature and impact of coaching. The findings provide new information about coaching, contributing to our evolving conceptualization of coaching and our understanding of what coaching clients want from the coaching process.

Definitions of Coaching

Coaching is, first and foremost, a relationship between two individuals. It is further clarified as a relationship in which one individual is seeking some type of help or assistance from another individual. The International Coach Federation (ICF), coach training schools, and the most recent coaching literature provide definitions of coaching that describe both personal and executive coaching. Commonalities include an emphasis on the relationship as the vehicle for the coaching process, facilitating client learning, improving client performance or effectiveness, and increasing client fulfillment (Coach University, 2002; Coaches Training Institute, 1996; Flaherty, 1999; Hudson Institute, 2002; International Coach Federation, 2002; Kilburg, 2000; New Ventures West, 2002; Pinchot and Pinchot, 2000; Schein, 2000; Whitworth, Kimsey-House, and Sandahl, 1998; Wilkins, 2000).

Although distinctions exist between personal and executive coaching, it is possible to develop a definition that describes both. Wilkins (2000) reported a similar conclusion: "Despite two separate contexts wherein coaching occurs, the overall understanding of what coaching is remains consistent" (p. 40). It appears, then, the practice of coaching can be described as a one-on-one, helping relationship that involves learning; coaching improves client effectiveness or performance, and increases the level of fulfillment of the client. Elements related to the active process of coaching can be added to this description, and include goal-setting, assessment, action, moving forward, transformation, reflection, and collaboration (Flaherty, 1999; Hudson, 1999; Kilburg, 2000; Sztucinski, 2001; Wilkins, 2000; Whitworth et al., 1998).

The Present Investigation

The general consensus in the coaching field, as the brief exploration above suggests, is that coaching is a process that aims to help clients feel better (be more fulfilled), do better (be more effective), and learn. Psychologists, counselors, and consultants also aim to help clients learn, increase effectiveness, and feel better. What then makes coaching unique?

The present investigation sought to address the essential nature of coaching by talking to the people who experience coaching first-hand. In-depth interviews with eight personal coaching clients who were currently engaged in a long-term coaching relationship with an experienced, certified coach were conducted. The study's guiding research question was: What is personal coaching from the perspective of the client?

Method

Selection

To limit variability because of differences in training, all referring coaches were certified by the Coaches Training Institute (CTI), an ICF-accredited coach training program. CTI was chosen as a certifying institution because of its location and because of my familiarity with its methods as a CTI-certified coach. All coaches who referred participants had either received their Master Coach Certification from the ICF, or met the following requirements designating sufficiency of experience: (a) completed at least three years of coaching since certification, (b) coached at least 30 clients since certification, and (c) provided at least 700 hours of direct coaching services.

Coaches who met the eligibility criteria referred participants to the study. Purposeful sampling was utilized to locate eight participants who were likely to be able to provide rich, detailed information about coaching. Participants were required to have experienced at least six months of coaching, and could not be trained coaches. Participants included four men and four women aged thirty through fifty; their occupations included authors, executives, artists, and managers.

Data Collection and Analysis

In-depth, in-person interviews were conducted with eight participants. An interview guide that addressed the guiding research question was used in each interview. Questions were open-ended, allowing participants to speak spontaneously about the aspects of their experience that were most meaningful to them.

The resulting database was analyzed using inductive methodology to develop a thick description of coaching from the client's perspective. Inductive analysis enables researchers to create rich descriptions of phenomena by engaging in a step-by-step process of uncovering dominant themes in the data (Patton, 1990). Each interview was analyzed separately in the following manner: (a) coding interview sections according to the research question they addressed; (b) identifying key words or phrases that recurred throughout an interview; (c) gathering key words into meaning units that described themes or patterns; (d) verifying that each key word was included in a meaning unit; (e) transforming meaning units into an outline of major themes and sub-themes; (f) reviewing original interviews and selecting quotations that described each major theme and sub-theme to verify accuracy; and (g) utilizing the themes' outline to develop a narrative summary statement for each participant.

After summary statements were developed, member checks were conducted to verify the accuracy of data analysis. Lincoln and Guba (1985) indicated that member checks enhance the credibility of qualitative research: ìThe member check, whereby data, analytic categories, interpretations, and conclusions are tested with members of those stake-holding groups from whom the data were originally collected, is the most crucial technique for establishing credibility (p. 314). Participants reviewed their narrative summary statements and provided feedback that was incorporated into their statements.

Once member checks had verified accuracy, cross-case data analysis was initiated. Summary statements were reviewed and major themes and sub-themes for every participant were identified. Cross-case charts were created that identified themes and sub-themes for all eight participants. Major themes were determined to be any component identified by five or more participants, and minor themes were determined to be any component identified by three or four participants.

Results

Thirteen major themes were identified that address the nature and impact of personal coaching (see Table 1). Minor themes describing coaching, the coach's role, and coaching impact are reported in Tables 2, 3, and 4. All names have been changed to protect participant confidentiality.

The Coaching Process

A number of major themes described the coaching process. All participants agreed that coaching involves identifying specific goals. This theme was the most robust, with all participants discussing how coaching helps to clarify what they want professionally or personally. Josh reported: So much of coaching can be about goals and goal work… you set your goals and you grow into them.

Many participants also reported that coaching involves discovering what's important at a deep, personal level. Eleanor stated that coaching: [helps] you develop who you want to become….It's…like a blueprint for your life. Allen, who started coaching because of its practical focus on work, was surprised by the soulful nature of coaching: Who are you, what's important, how do you want to live your life are questions you deal with in coaching. Leanne, who started coaching because she wanted help finding a job, was also surprised at how coaching involved learning to listen to her inner voice: …it speaks to the deepest part of…who I am or what I want…instead of just the next job. It's…about…whole purpose in life.

For these participants, coaching involves delving into profound questions about their inner selves as well as practical questions about their goals. Participants described the coaching relationship as an essential part of the coaching process. They explicitly identified trust and support as important characteristics of the relationship.

Eleanor: I feel like I've known her my whole life, and I trust her implicitly.
Kayla: It's a never-ending support. It's like always having somebody there.

Participants reported feeling cared about or loved by their coaches, and some described how coaching provides a unique relationship in which they can be completely themselves.

> Nanette: …coaching was always the place I could go, where I knew that I could be totally honest about every other facet of my life…no matter what was happening in my life…[my coach] could hear it, not judge it, and move me to the next level.
> Allen: It's very safe…I don't experience anything in the relationship that makes me feel like I need to be other than who I am. That's a very unusual experience…a very powerful experience. It is unconditional acceptance in some more existential way than…romantic love or parental love… The strength and unique positive quality of the coaching relationship clearly emerged as a defining feature of the coaching experience.

Many participants reported that coaching involves changing their mental views of various issues and challenging times. Nanette described how her coach encourages her to shift her perspective to see the big picture.

> Nanette: …then he asks me this big question where I have to…climb up on some kind of ladder…and see over [the issue]. I call it getting in my helicopter and seeing the bigger terrain, rather than getting stuck in the details.

Other participants described how their coaches provide them with feedback that increases their mental flexibility and their options. Gus, a high-level executive, turned to his coach, rather than peers, when he was looking for feedback, because coaching gives you a different perspective.

Participants reported that coaching follows their agendas, and focuses on the present and future rather than the past. Nanette explained that she determines the focus of coaching sessions: [My coach] always puts the ball in my court. Seven participants had worked with psychotherapists, and they distinguished coaching from psychotherapy in terms of coaching's focus on the present and future.

> Nanette: [My coach]…doesn't monkey around and waste…time talking about stuff that's not really key for what's happening at that moment.
> Allen: It is less about why are things the way they are…than what is the way they are…and what way do you want them to be.
> Kayla: I've been in therapy before where…hour-long sessions for months, and I get more done in a half an hour with a coach. It's because it is about positive things and the future, and moving forward, and it is different from…a therapy session, even though we do touch on some [therapeutic] things and issues.

The participants also reported that coaching promotes client accountability and identifies and challenges internal barriers to success. Gus continues with coaching because, when I'm held accountable for something, [it] has a greater chance of getting done."

Leanne explained: "[Coaches] operate at a higher level, about what is it that you want and what gets in your way, and helping you remove what gets in your way." These clients reported that helping them stay accountable and overcome emotional blocks helped them to reach their goals.

The Coach's Role

Several major themes emerged regarding the coach's role. Participants reported that coaches provide validation for who they are and what they have accomplished. They reported that their coaches remind them of their strengths and believe in them wholeheartedly:

> Leanne: …one of the things she does for me is feed back to me some of my competencies that I don't always believe in…that is very helpful, and gives a great boost to a person who at times has stopped believing…in her ability to do something or to be something.
> Josh: [My coach] sees my better self…He remembers the me that is a good [artist], a good father, a good husband, trying to do good in the world…He remembers the self that is creative…and focused. And accomplished.
> Kayla: She just knows me better than [I know myself]…And she believes in me more than [I believe in myself].

These participants indicated that coaches provide validation for clients' deepest selves, as well as clients' concrete achievements.

Participants identified the ability to listen and ask thought-provoking questions as key coaching skills. Josh explained: "What the coach needs to do first, primarily, and most… is listen." Leanne said, "Sometimes [my coach asks] me a question and that will just lead to an entire hour's worth of conversation." Eleanor identified the link between skilled listening and questioning: "The questioning is extremely important, but if you're listening you know what the questions are."

The Impact of Coaching

Several major themes emerged regarding the coach's role. Participants reported that coaching promoted learning and self-discovery, and they developed a deeper understanding of their desires, their behavior, and their impact on others. Several participants spoke about a stronger connection with their "intuition":

> Allen: …what I have been coached on is how to be in touch with myself. How to have this…conversation with myself in an ongoing way, so that I can live in a way that's…an expression of who I am, consistent with my soul…
> Leanne: …what coaching has done is to very gradually force me…to pay attention to this voice that has probably been there for years and has never been allowed any legitimacy.

Participants also reported experiencing success in one or more areas of their lives as a result of coaching. Some participants succeeded at work, receiving promotions or changing jobs, while others succeeded in implementing personal goals such as buying a house or exercising regularly. Eleanor discussed how coaching helped her overcome self-defeating beliefs and win a promotion: "…it was my belief systems that were in the way… Because once I got the belief systems out of the way, I got the promotion."

As a result of coaching, the participants felt more positive about themselves. Josh reported that coaching ìhas really allowed me to feel a good deal more successful". Leanne described how coaching helps her to remember her abilities:

> Leanne: …when I'm away from [my coach]…something will come up where I have a question in my brain. Am I capable of this? And is this who I really am? And memories of those conversations with her about what she sees as my strengths will come back, and reinforce [me] at that moment.

These participants reported that coaching enabled them to believe in themselves to a greater degree, and improved their self-esteem.

Limitations

Because this study aimed to understand what coaching is when it is succeeding, only experienced coaches were allowed to refer clients as participants. Thus, the present study did not provide an optimal lens for viewing the failures or pitfalls of coaching. Because participants were purposefully selected rather than randomly selected, the results' generalizability may be limited. In particular, because the study explored coaching as practiced by coaches trained at one institution (CTI), the results may not describe coaching as experienced by clients of coaches trained at other institutions.

Discussion

The current findings indicated that, in large measure, the participants experienced coaching as it has been described in the existing literature. In particular, these clients experienced coaching as a process that involved both action and learning. They moved forward in their lives through goal-setting and accomplishment, and they learned a great deal about themselves in the process. They became more aware of their desires and needs, they learned how to shift their perspectives on challenging issues, and they learned how to identify and overcome their internal saboteurs. Most of the literature on coaching emphasized that coaching involves action and performance results, and much of the literature described client learning as an important element of the coaching process (Coach University, 2002; Creane, 2002; Coaches Training Institute, 1996; Flaherty, 1999; Hudson Institute, 2002; International Coach Federation, 2002; Kilburg, 2000; New Ventures West, 2002; Pinchot and Pinchot, 2000; Schein, 2000; Whitworth, et al., 1998; Wilkins, 2000). Thus, the findings regarding action and learning substantiate the existing literature, and support the conceptualizations of coaching discussed earlier in the article.

One finding in particular appeared to extend the existing literature on coaching. These participants spoke at length about their relationship with their coaches. The personal connections they experienced with their coaches were powerful and uniquely intimate, while still experienced as professional. Although some authors on coaching discuss the coaching relationship, the relationship is usually considered as the vehicle for the coaching goals of learning, action, and effectiveness. These participants, however, spoke about the depth and transformative potential of the coaching relationship as a defining feature of the coaching process, and as a benefit to them regardless of the content or outcome of coaching.

Significantly, two research studies that used qualitative methods to explore coaching identified the coaching relationship as essential to the coaching process. Wilkins (2000) identified the coaching relationship as one of three "cornerstones" in her grounded theory model of personal coaching. She explained that the relationship was characterized by "unwavering support, honesty, affirmation, awareness, action, and truth telling" (p. 129). Sztucinski (2001), who explored coaching from the perspective of executive coaching clients, identified the "bond with the coach" as one of seven essential elements that describe the coaching experience. She stated, "The deep sense of seemingly unconditional caring and support given by the coach to the executive was critical to the overall success of the coaching experience" (p. 184). These findings, together with the current results, indicated that the coaching relationship is powerful and is experienced as a significant source of support for clients.

While much of the research on psychotherapy has focused on the significance of the therapeutic alliance and the importance of the therapeutic relationship to the overall success of psychotherapy, very little research has been conducted on the importance of the coaching relationship to the overall process and success of coaching. Further research is warranted in order to assess the degree to which the nature and quality of the coaching alliance affects the client's coaching experience and the ultimate outcomes of the coaching process.

Another comparison to therapy emerged as clients discussed coaching's focus on the present and future rather than the past. Seven participants had current or past experiences of psychotherapy. Although all participants spoke favorably about psychotherapy, they indicated that coaching provided them with a unique opportunity to understand their current lives and desires and plan for their futures. They reported that past issues occasionally arose in coaching, but they were handled differently than they would have been in a therapeutic setting. Further research is required to explore the differences and similarities between coaching and psychotherapy, particularly how clients experience the two relationships and the differential impact that each service has on clients.

Another noteworthy finding is the emphasis that clients placed on validation. Participants reported that their coaches validated them for both their accomplishments and their innate personal qualities. Their coaches enabled them to see positive aspects of themselves that they would otherwise deny or minimize. Participants experienced this validation as transformative and unique to coaching. Their descriptions of validation suggested a deeper, more powerful experience of validation than was suggested in the literature on coaching to date. Further research is necessary to determine whether this finding holds true for other populations of coaching clients.

Further, these participants reported that coaching positively affected their sense of self. Future researchers may want to explore the relationship, if any, between validation in coaching and increased self-esteem in coaching clients. Findings regarding the effects of psychotherapy on client self-esteem will provide a useful comparison for any research into the relationship between coaching and self-esteem.

As mentioned earlier, coaching is an emerging profession that is still developing a coherent narrative to describe itself. Given this, the language these participants used to describe coaching is particularly interesting. They clearly articulated that coaching involves and results in goal identification, accountability, learning, action, and effectiveness–all factors discussed in the limited coaching literature. The participants, however, also described coaching as something more. They described coaching as a "soulful," heart-opening process that helped them connect with their deepest desires, their greatest strengths, and their overall life purposes. Several participants chose coaching because of its ìpracticalî reputation, and were surprised by how the coaching process required them to pay attention to their inner world in a whole new way. These findings again beg the question of how coaching is different from psychotherapy (which also focuses clients inward), but the findings also raise the question of how coaching manages to be both practical and soulful, both results-oriented and transformative. This duality, in particular, appears to set coaching apart, and certainly warrants further investigation.

Conclusions

Personal coaching is gaining widespread popularity in the United States and around the globe. New practices or professions do not emerge and thrive unless they address the specific needs of individuals or communities. It seems likely that coaching emerged as a result of a need that was not being met by traditional helping relationships, such as psychotherapy or consulting. While coaching deals with psychological issues such as belief systems, barriers to success, interpersonal bonding, and self-esteem, it does this in a way that is particular to coaching itself. While coaching, like consulting, focuses on goals and results, it again does this in a way that is unique to coaching. The success of coaching as a fledgling profession demonstrates that individuals want and are willing to pay for a helping relationship that bridges the worlds of psychological transformation and goal-oriented consulting.

Although coaches hail from a variety of backgrounds, coaches fundamentally share a common belief that has both shaped and defined the coaching profession: an unwavering faith in the ability of human beings to change, grow, and lead fulfilling and effective lives. As coaching becomes a more established discipline, coaching researchers and practitioners have an enormous opportunity in the coming years to define this emerging practice so that it continues to address the unique needs and concerns of twenty-first century clients.

References

Brotman, L. E., Liberi, W. P., & Wasylyshyn, K.M. (1998). Executive coaching: The need for standards of competence. *Consulting Psychology Journal, 50*(1), 40-45. Coach University. (2002; Date unavailable). What is coaching all about? Retrieved November 4, 2002 from http://www.coachinc.com/CoachU/Become%20A%20Coach/FAQ/common%20questions/group%20a/default.asp?s=1

Coaches Training Institute. (1996). *Coaches Training Institute Course Manual.* San Rafael, CA: The Coaches Training Institute.

Coaches Training Institute. (2000). *Coaches Training Institute Course Manual.* San Rafael, CA: The Coaches Training Institute.

Creane, V. (2002). *An exploratory study of personal coaching from the client's perspective.* (Unpublished doctoral dissertation, San Francisco, CA, California Institute of Integral Studies).

Flaherty, J. (1999). *Evoking excellence in others.* Boston, MA: Butterworth-Heinemann.

Garman, A., Whiston, D., & Zlatoper, K. (2000) Media perceptions of executive coaching and the formal preparation of coaching. *Consulting Psychology Journal, 52,* 201-205.

Hudson, F. M. (1999). *The handbook of coaching: A comprehensive resource guide for managers, executives, consultants, and human resource professionals.* San Francisco, CA: Jossey-Bass.

Hudson Institute. (2002; Date unavailable). Frequently asked questions about HI's Coach Certification Program. Retrieved November 4, 2002 from http://www.hudsoninstitute.com/pages/coach_faqs.html

International Coach Federation. (2002; Date unavailable). About coaching. Retrieved December 1, 2002 from http://www.coachfederation.org/aboutcoaching/index.htm

Kilburg, R. R. (1996). Toward a conceptual understanding and definition of executive coaching. *Consulting Psychology Journal, 48*(2), 134-144.

Kilburg, R. R. (2000). *Executive coaching: Developing managerial wisdom in a world of chaos.* Washington, DC: American Psychological Association.

Lincoln, Y. S. & Guba, E. G. (1985). *Naturalistic inquiry.* Beverly Hills, CA: Sage Publications, Inc.

New Ventures West. (2002; Date unavailable). Coaching: a competence for all times —especially now. Retrieved November 4, 2002 from http://www.newventureswest.com/

Patton, M. Q. (1990). *Qualitative evaluation and research methods,* Second Edition. Newbury Park, CA: Sage Publications, Inc.

Pinchot, E. & Pinchot, G. (2000). Roots and boundaries of executive coaching. In M. Goldsmith, L. Lyons, & A. Freas, (Eds.), *Coaching for leadership: How the world's greatest coaches help leaders learn* (pp. 43-64). San Francisco, CA: Jossey-Bass/Pfeiffer.

Schein, E. H. (2000). Coaching and consultation: are they the same? In M. Goldsmith, L. Lyons, & A. Freas, (Eds.), *Coaching for leadership: How the world's greatest coaches help leaders learn* (pp. 65-73). San Francisco, CA: Jossey-Bass/Pfeiffer.

Sztucinski, K. (2001). *The nature of executive coaching: An exploration of the executive's experience.* (Unpublished doctoral dissertation, Washington, DC, George Washington University).

Whitworth, L., Kimsey-House, H., & Sandahl, P. (1998). *Co-active coaching: New skills for coaching people toward success in work and life.* Palo Alto, CA: Davies-Black Publishing.

Wilkins, B. (2000). *A grounded theory study of personal coaching.* (Unpublished doctoral dissertation, Missoula, MT, University of Montana

*Valerie Creane, Psy.D. is a therapist, coach, and group facilitator. As a psychologist, Dr. Creane conducts collaborative psychological assessments, a unique 360-degree process that integrates the principles of coaching into comprehensive mental health evaluations. As a coach, Dr. Creane integrates her clinical understanding of the depth and power of the human psyche into her coaching practice. Dr. Creane has delivered workshops on team-building, communication, coaching skills and stress management for for-profit and non-profit organizations. She earned a doctorate in Clinical Psychology, Psy.D., from California Institute of Integral Studies. She is a Certified Professional Co-Active Coach through Coaches Training Institute and is a graduate, Co-Active Space Leadership Program. Dr. Creane is a member of the International Coach Federation and American Psychological Association. Contact: vcreane@epiccoaching.com.*

A Heuristic Inquiry Into the Impact of a Vipassana Meditation Practice on Executive Coaching

Barbara Braham

Heuristics is a type of phenomenological research in which meaning is discovered through a process of self-search. This paper describes a heuristic study designed to investigate the impact of the Theravada Buddhist meditation practice vipassana (also known as mindfulness meditation) on executive coaching. The literature reveals that most executive coaches rely on their legacy field, whether that is psychology, organizational development or some other field, as the theoretical foundation for their practice. Coaches also bring a personal philosophy, or worldview, to their coaching. This study explores how the worldview that emerges after years of vipassana meditation impacts executive coaching.

Following a personal heuristic inquiry, 90 minute face-to-face interviews were conducted with seven Caucasian executive coaches from across the United States who had had a daily vipassana meditation practice for 10 to 23 years. Three coaches were female; four were male. The coaches came from educational backgrounds including psychology, organizational development, business and education. All but one person had been coaching for at least five years.

In individual interviews, coaches were asked to describe their executive coaching practice, vipassana meditation practice and the impact (if any) of their vipassana practice on their coaching. The data clustered into four themes:

The Practice: Mindfulness while coaching
The View: Insights from the practice
Living the View: Integrating the practice into work and life
Being the View

Theme one describes how mindfulness is used as a tool to be present and self-aware while coaching. Theme two explains how insights gained from meditating create a worldview that shapes how the coach listens, understands and intervenes. Living the View describes how the worldview is integrated into personal and work life. In theme four, the coaches have greater access to their intuition and are able to embody the worldview without consciously thinking about it.

No one can deny that in the past eight to ten years executive coaching has stepped into the foreground with the publication of a flood of articles in professional journals and business magazines (Garman, Whiston and Zlatoper, 2000), books, and the creation of schools to train executive coaches. Despite all of this attention, executive coaching is without an agreed upon theory base (Grant 2001; Witherspoon and White, 1997).

Practitioners rely upon their legacy field, whether organizational development, psychology, management, education or something else, for their theoretical grounding (Sherman and Freas, 2004) and adopt a variety of tools and techniques from the other disciplines into their coaching practice. For example, coaches look to organizational development for an understanding of organizational systems (Senge, 1990), organizational culture (Schein, 1992), organizational change (Argyris and Schon, 1996), and small group behavior (French and Bell, 1999). From psychology, coaches find theory for assessing the strengths and weaknesses of an individual leader (Seligman, 2002), developmental levels (Kegan, 1995; Laske, 2004), and emotional intelligence (Goleman, 1997).

Coaches also come to the coaching engagement with a worldview, or a philosophy (Goldrich, 2004). While some coaches are aware of the philosophy that influences their coaching, for most their philosophy is tacit. Yet it is the worldview that influences which theories a coach relies upon in practice. Using psychological theories as an example, a coach who holds a tragic or pessimistic worldview will be drawn to deficit based psychological theories whereas a coach with a more optimistic worldview will be drawn to humanistic and positive psychology theories.

In a review of the literature, there were only a few authors who were transparent about their worldview (Flaherty 1996; Goldrich, 2004). "It is my premise that coaching is a principle-shaped ontological stance and not a series of techniques" (Flaherty, 1996, p. 13). Goldrich (2004) writes "Today considerable evidence exists to indicate that you cannot provide feedback or ask a question without communicating a point of view… I concluded that, for me, ethical practice means knowing and being clear to clients about how I believe things work (the universe, businesses, human beings etc.) and about the philosophies I am communicating about the most effective way to be… " (p. 7). Marshall Goldsmith (2004) talks about his Zen practice and how that worldview influences his coaching by stating, "My coaching practice involves a lot of Buddhist thought including: letting go of the past, realizing we are all interdependent, accepting that change is always happening and accepting 'what is.'"

This researcher was interested in what the Buddhist worldview might contribute to the theory and practice of executive coaching. "The question has often been asked: Is Buddhism a religion or a philosophy? It does not matter what you call it. Buddhism remains what it is whatever label you may put on it" (Rahula, 1959, p. 4). In this study, Buddhism is approached not as a religion, but as a philosophy, or worldview. As Batchelor (1997) and Kabat-Zinn (1994) have pointed out, the Dharma (the teachings of the Buddha) requires no religious beliefs, and therefore creates no conflict with the personal religious beliefs of a coach or an executive. Further, the religion of Buddhism is non-theistic.

The Dharma entered the West in a significant way in the 1970's. Since then psychology (and psychoanalysis in particular) has been experimenting with the integration of Buddhism into psychotherapy (Rubin, 1999; Safran, 2003). If the Dharma can enrich therapy, might it also enrich executive coaching?

Research Question

Heuristics is a type of phenomenological research in which the researcher uses a process of self-search and self-discovery to uncover and disclose the meaning of an experience. This paper describes a heuristic inquiry into the impact, if any, of a Theravada Buddhist meditation practice called vipassana, sustained over a period of years, on executive coaching. Vipassana is a Sanskrit word that means insight, and is commonly known as mindfulness meditation.

The word impact is used to mean the effect of vipassana on the coach and how that, in turn, affects the coaching. Impact is not used to imply coaching effectiveness, or coaching outcomes. The phrase daily vipassana meditation practice, sustained over a period of years is used to limit this study to dedicated (daily) practitioners who are not new to the practice, but rather are experienced practitioners (sustained over a period of years).

The Dharma Worldview

The teachings of the Buddha that were explored as fundamental to a worldview for coaching were the Four Noble Truths: suffering, its origin, its cessation, and the way leading to its cessation. The way leading to its cessation is called the Noble Eightfold Path which includes right view, right intention, right speech, right action, right livelihood, right effort, right mindfulness and right concentration (Nanamoli & Bodhi, 1995; Rahula, 1959). The emphasis in this study was on one aspect of the Noble Eightfold Path: Right Mindfulness.

Mindfulness Meditation

The practice of vipassana, or mindfulness meditation, is simple, although not easy. You sit on a chair or cushion, close your eyes and focus your attention on your breath. Placing undivided attention on the in-and-out flow of the breath helps keep the meditator in the present moment and not the past or the future. "It is an exclusive state of mind. Everything is excluded but the object on which we're concentrating. When we notice that our attention has wandered, we return our attention to the breath. Concentrative meditation cultivates a high degree of mental focus" (Rubin 1999, p. 2).

As you practice vipassana, you gain insight and wisdom to see things as they really are. "When we use this phrase [seeing things as they really are] in reference to insight gained from our meditation, what we mean is not seeing things superficially with our regular eyes, but seeing things with wisdom as they are in themselves .... Mindfulness practice is the practice of being 100 percent honest with ourselves. When we watch our own mind and body, we notice certain things that are unpleasant to realize. As we do not like them, we try to reject them. What are the things we do not like? We do not like to detach ourselves from loved ones or to live with unloved ones. We include not only people, places, and material things into our likes and dislikes, but opinions, ideas, beliefs, and decisions as well. We do not like what naturally happens to us. We do not like, for instance, growing old, becoming sick, becoming weak, or showing our age… We do not like someone pointing out our faults for we take great pride in ourselves. We do not like someone to be wiser than we are, for we are deluded about ourselves (Gunaratana, 1991, pp. 51-54).

The Method: Heuristic Inquiry

The word heuristic comes from the Greek word heuriskein which means to find or to discover. "From the beginning, and throughout an investigation, heuristic research involves self-search, self-dialogue, and self discovery; the research question and the methodology flow out of inner awareness, meaning, and inspiration" (Moustakas, 1990, p. 11).

In executive coaching, it is not uncommon to invite a leader to live with a question, rather than trying to answer it right away. The coach guides the leader into the paradox "The question is the answer." Similarly, the process of a heuristic study "requires a subjective process of reflecting, exploring, sifting, and elucidating the nature of the phenomena under investigation" (Douglass and Moustakas,1985, p. 40). The researcher lives in the research question in six specific ways. Those six ways (or phases), which constitute the basic research design, are initial engagement, immersion, incubation, illumination, explication, and creative synthesis.

In heuristic research the term co-researcher is used rather than the word subject. After immersion and inquiry into the experience of having a daily vipassana meditation practice and an executive coaching practice, the researcher creates open-ended questions (Table 1) to be used with co-researchers as a framework for dialogue.

Table 1

Will you describe your executive/leader coaching practice?
What theory or theories inform your practice?
Would you describe your practice of the Dharma?
What is your experience of being a student of the Dharma and an executive coach?
In what ways does your practice of the Dharma impact your coaching practice?
What do you observe about your use of self during coaching that may be influenced by your meditation practice?
How does the Dharma influence how you listen to your clients?
Would you talk about any relationship you observe between the worldview of the Dharma and your coaching practice?
Are there ways in which you feel your coaching practice may be different from other coaches who are not students of the Dharma?
Would you describe ways that your meditation practice has shaped how you conceptualize coaching?

Selection of Co-researchers

Two criteria were used to select co-researchers. The first criterion was that the individual had had a daily vipassana meditation practice for at least 10 years in the Theravada Buddhist tradition. Ten years of practice was chosen to correspond with the length of the researcher's practice.

The second criterion was that the individual coached executives or leaders. There were no requirements as to how long they had been an executive coach, or their particular approach to executive coaching.

Summary of Co-researchers

Co-researcher	Coaching Method (F - Face-to-Face) (V - Virtual) (B - Both)	Age	Location	Education	Coach Training	Years of Coaching	Years of Practicing Vipassana
Barbara	B	53	Midwest	B.A. - Psychology B.S.W. - Social Work M.S.W. - Social Work	Yes	10	11
Betsy*	F	54	East	B.A. - Psychology M.A. - Counseling Ph.D. - Counseling	No	10	10
David	B	52	East	B.A. - Social Science M.A. - City Planning M.S. - Behavioral Science	No	25	15
Eric	B	38	West	B.A. - International Business	No	7	19
Jean	F	56	Midwest	B.A. - Education M.P.A.- Public Administration	Yes	1	11
Peter	B	58	Midwest	B.S. - Communication M.A. - Communication M.S. - Behavioral Science Ph.D. - Communication	No	25	14
Sandra	V	68	West	B.A. - Education	Yes	9	14
Steve	F	51	West	M.S.W. - Social Work	No	5	23

* Indicates the only co-researcher who was an internal coach.

Table 2

Because it was difficult to find people who met these two criteria, there was no attempt to balance the cohort with regard to race or gender. The cohort was made up of four men and three women; all were Caucasian. The co-researchers came from across the U. S; two were from the east coast, two were from the Midwest, and three were from California. Table 2 summarizes the demographics of the co-researchers and the researcher.

Three of the seven co-researchers did not have an educational background in counseling, psychology, or organizational development. Two of those three attended coach specific training (CoachU and the Gestalt Institute of Cleveland). The third individual lived in a spiritual community that was also a teaching order, and as a teacher practiced many coach-like behaviors.

The majority of the coaches (five) do their work face-to-face with leaders, with some telephone or e-mail support between visits. Two co-researchers have a practice that is primarily virtual (e-mail and telephone).

Frederick Hudson (1999) believed that to be a coach an individual needed 40 years of life experience. The cohort seems to affirm his premise. Five co-researchers and myself were in their 50's, one was in her 60's, and one was in his late 30's.

Data Collection and Analysis

Because both executive coaching and the Dharma are large topics, an interview guide (Table 1) was used to create a structure and boundary for the interviews. "The interview guide simply serves as a basic checklist during the interview to make sure that all relevant topics are covered…. The interviewer is thus required to adapt both the wording and the sequence of questions to specific respondents in the context of the actual interview" (Patton, 1990, p. 280). The face-to-face interviews lasted between 60 and 90 minutes and were tape-recorded with permission.

The interviews resulted in 255 typed pages of transcript. Each interview was summarized into an individual depiction, which in a couple of pages captures the essence of the interview using the co-researchers own words. After an individual depiction was written, the co-researcher was asked for a telephone interview to verify the accuracy of the depiction.

The process of identifying themes began once all of the individual depictions had been accepted. This was done by reading each depiction and capturing on note cards what seemed to be the critical themes. After all seven depictions were reviewed, the cards were sorted into related clusters. After periods of incubation the cards were re-clustered until four themes emerged. The four themes are:

- The Practice: Mindfulness while coaching
- The View: Insights from the practice
- Living the View: Integrating the practice into work and life
- Being the View

Theme 1: The Practice: Mindfulness While Coaching

At its most fundamental, mindfulness is about stopping, pausing and bringing yourself into the present moment. As thoughts arise you use a technique called "noting" in which you simply name or note "thinking, thinking" (Goldstein, 1976). Noting can also be used with bodily sensations and emotions. The practice teaches you to meet each moment as it is without pushing it away or trying to cling to it. Thus, you gradually learn how to be with the present moment regardless of whether it is pleasant, unpleasant or neutral.

These co-researchers frequently bring mindfulness into an executive coaching conversation. The coach is not talking about her mindfulness practice with the executive; she is practicing mindfulness in the midst of the conversation. Notice in the following quotes from interviews how mindfulness has enabled the coach to be, in Bowen's (2000-2004) words, "a non-anxious presence."

> I think a lot of it [coaching] is about mindfulness, and just sitting there aware and equanimous. It's not getting caught up in their particular storm of the moment, and that is a huge value to my clients. They can storm in my presence and pretty soon it passes and we can still sit there and go, "OK, so what's beyond that?" I use my sensations to monitor myself, and I use them a lot as guides in the conversation.

> One way that the meditation practice has influenced my work, is that it allows me to step back 1/8 inch from the anxiety of the other individual or group. People are so anxious. If I can step back a little, I can see something bigger than their anxiety or their demands. I learned about the role of anxiety from Bowen, but the cushion gives you the skill to manage your anxiety.

One of the factors that facilitates change and makes transformation possible is the capacity of the executive coach to "be present" with the executive (O'Neill, 2000).

The International Coach Federation lists "coaching presence" as one of their eleven core competencies. The practice of mindfulness while coaching enables the coach to be present with the "full catastrophe" (to use a phrase coined by Anthony Quinn in the movie Zorba the Greek and popularized by Kabat-Zinn, 1990) of emotions, feelings and thoughts of an executive without needing to change, fix or push away any of it.

The practice is about 'being with.' It gives me a stance that allows me to be with the other person with a certain kind of transparency, authenticity and quality of engagement. I am able to 'be with' because the practice has taught me how to empty myself. I have learned how to recognize a thought and set it aside when I am sitting. When I'm with a coaching client I can acknowledge my projections and set them aside just as I would with a thought when I'm meditating.

Theme 2: The View: Insights from the Practice

When one practices meditation over time (years), one gradually learns to still the mind. With this quieting, insight can arise. It is personally experienced universal insights that gradually shape a worldview. While these insights are rarely shared directly with a coaching partner, the resultant worldview shapes what is heard, how one intervenes and the stance that one takes in the world. In the following excerpt a co-researcher describes the impact of one insight — interconnectedness — on his work with others.

> The foundation in my own experience is that everything is interdependent and interconnected. When I am working with the client we are interconnected; I take that for granted. To the degree that I can be mindful and present, to the degree that I can practice well, that's the degree to which I can serve them well. I can be closer to them than they can be to themselves by virtue of being in that interconnectedness.

With continued vipassana practice, compassion for oneself and others begins to expand. Compassion, in the Buddhist worldview, is a natural outpouring for oneself and others when there is insight into the universal truth of suffering. The gradual accumulation of insights leads to the arising of wisdom. Wisdom, in the Buddhist worldview, is the ability to see universal insights. In these quotes co-researchers talk about how they view wisdom and compassion in their coaching work.

> I bring compassion to my work because I am engaging with human beings on the journey of their life. It happens to be called business, or leadership, or sales or whatever, but this is their life. And I am aware that I am engaging in something pretty precious.

> Wisdom and compassion are my keys. Where I really feel connected, is around wisdom and compassion. So I bring that to my clients. What I feel gets lived out in me, from my head and my heart, is what I know from my practice in terms of opening my heart and clearing my mind. That's what I bring to my work now. And that's what presence is to me.

Theme 3: Living the View: Integrating the Practice into Work and Life

As the emerging worldview becomes more apparent, there is a natural desire to live one's life congruent with that view. This is what the Buddha referred to as Right Livelihood in the Eightfold Path. The vipassana practitioner wants to live the Dharma and not simply talk about the Dharma. Living the View means integrating the Dharma into one's life, and that includes one's work life. There is a seamlessness between the meditation cushion and day-to-day activities. Thus, while a co-researcher may define executive coaching as building capacity, or helping a leader achieve specific goals, that coach will also tell you that the highest aim is to alleviate suffering – the First Noble Truth. Notice in the following quotes how Living the View and coaching have in some ways become synonymous.

> The most important asset in this work is my practice. The emotional intelligence framework is a tool. The gestalt concepts provide some structure, but my practice is the core of what I'm doing in the coaching sessions.

> The cushion is a rehearsal place, but the practice is life. I am only as good a coach as I am practicing in that moment.

> I think everything I do as a coach, all of my actions, are a result of the Dharma more than any other influence in my life. It always feels good to be able to take some of what I have experienced [on the cushion] and bring it out there. I mean, that's what it's all about; it's not just about sitting on the cushion.

Theme 4: Being the View

This theme is analogous to the stage of learning known as the unconscious competent. The co-researcher does not need to consciously live the view, or integrate the view into their life. Now they can embody, or be, the view. In theme four the individual does not even have an attachment to the view. There is no need to hold on to anything, whether it's a coaching model or the Dharma itself. From years of practice and personal inquiry the meditator has developed a deep trust in the process of unfolding. This trust is often experienced and expressed as an expanded intuitive capacity. The intuitive capacity was described by several co-researchers as influencing how they listen.

> I don't listen for content. I listen for what's underlying. I listen for the music more than the words. My ability to do this has been influenced by my practice. I tried to hear what is being asked for at the deepest level as opposed to what is being asked for in the words the person is using.

> When I'm listening to clients, the guiding principle for me is the basic question, "What do you need from me right now, in this moment, to further the process?" It's not even what's needed from me. It's just "What's needed to move this process forward in a constructive way?" I think it has taken 20 years of practice before

I could trust myself to just listen for what's needed. It takes me out of ego identification to just being open to the field, and to allow the field to elicit a skillful response.

Discussion and Summary

This study was the result of my own deep curiosity about how my vipassana meditation practice was influencing my executive coaching work. I wondered if what I brought to the coaching conversation from the cushion was unique to me, or if it was characteristic of all vipassana practicing coaches. Thus, this study was designed to inquire not only into my experience but also into the experience of other vipassana practicing coaches. Every co-researcher stated unequivocally that the Dharma was the source of their worldview, and that the Dharma impacted their coaching work.

The data from the interviews revealed that for this cohort a vipassana practice impacted coaching in four specific ways. First, vipassana trains the practitioner to bring the quality of presence cultivated on the cushion into daily life. All of the coaches used mindfulness to be fully present and engaged with their coaching clients. The ability to be in the present moment, undistracted, lends itself to creating the kind of relationship that Hubble, Duncan, and Miller (1999) said accounts for 30% of the positive outcomes in therapy. It seems reasonable to assume that this kind of presence in a coaching relationship would also contribute to positive outcomes. In addition, the coaches in this study spoke about their ability to be a "non-anxious" presence while they were with a coaching partner; this capacity was strengthened by their sitting practice.

Second, the insights gained from the practice of vipassana have direct application to executive coaching. For example, the insight of interconnectedness helps the coach use a systems perspective in their work with executives. The insight of wisdom is critical in helping executives make distinctions between knowledge (knowing what to do) and wisdom (knowing when to do it).

Third, the Dharma provides a bigger framework for working with an executive than personal effectiveness, professional development, or business results. That bigger goal is contained in the Four Noble Truths: the elimination of suffering. A bigger framework may or may not be of interest to the coaching partner; however, it will likely provide a deep sense of purpose and meaning for the coach. When work, personal life and the Dharma are integrated, authenticity is the result.

Fourth, years of sustained practice yielded increased intuitive capacity. The co-researchers spoke of trusting themselves and their own inner voice. They also spoke about an ability to sense more fully what the client actually needed rather than what the client was necessarily asking for in words. Further research is needed to determine if this quality of listening may be what Torbert (2004), Kegan (1995), and others attribute to post conventional stages of adult development.

This study is the first to investigate the impact of a worldview on executive coaching. Further studies are needed to inquire into other worldviews and their impact on executive coaching. Outcome studies are also needed to assess if the impact the vipassana practicing coaches feel they're having is validated by their clients. Laske, Stober, and Edwards (2004) have proposed that executive coaching needs an interdisciplinary theory. I concur, and believe that worldview or philosophy needs to be an integral part of an interdisciplinary theory.

References

Argyris, C., & Schon, D. A. (1996). *Organizational learning II: Theory, method, and practice.* Reading, MA: Addison-Wesley.

Batchelor, S. (1997). *Buddhism without beliefs: A contemporary guide to awakening.* New York, NY: Riverhead Books.

Bowen Center for the Study of the Family 2000-2004. Bowen theory. Retrieved August 8, 2004, from http://www.thebowencenter.org/pages/theory.html.

Douglass, B. & Moustakas, C. (1985). Heuristic inquiry: The internal search to know. *Journal of Humanistic Psychology, 25*(3), 39-55.

Flaherty, J. (1996). *Coaching: Evoking excellence in others.* Boston: Butterworth Heinmann.

French, W., & Bell, C. (1999). *Organization development: Behavior science interventions for organization improvement* (6th ed.). New York: Prentice Hall.

Garman, A. N., Whiston, D. L., & Zlatoper, K. W. (2000, Summer). Media perceptions of executive coaching and the formal preparation of coaches. *Consulting Psychology Journal: Practice & Research, 52*(3), 201-205.

Goldrich, J. (2004). Coaching: A map of the territory. In P. Y. Griffin (Ed.), *The foundations of coaching* (pp. 1-17). Orefield, PA: Consulting Today.

Goldsmith, M. (2004). Zen and business. Retrieved January 8, 2005 from http://www.zenandbusinessnewsletter.com/Summer%202004%20Newsletter.htm.

Goldstein, J. (1976). *The experience of insight: A simple and direct guide to Buddhist meditation.* Boston, MA: Shambhala.

Goleman, D. P. (1997). *Emotional intelligence.* New York, NY: Bantam Books.

Grant, A. (2001). Towards a psychology of coaching. Retrieved December 20, 2004 from University of Sydney, Coaching Psychology Unit Web site: http://www.psych.usyd.edu.au/psychcoach/AMG_PhD_2001.pdf.

Gunaratana, V. H. (1991). *Mindfulness in plain English.* Boston, MA: Wisdom Publications.

Hubble, M. A., Duncan, B. L.& Miller, S.D. (Eds.). (1999). *The heart & soul of change: What works in therapy.* Washington, DC: American Psychological Association.

Hudson, F. M. (1999). *The handbook of coaching: A comprehensive resource guide for managers, executives, consultants, and HR.* San Francisco, CA: Jossey-Bass.

Kabat-Zinn, J. (1990). *Full catastrophe living: Using the wisdom of your body and mind to face stress, pain, and illness.* New York, NY: Dell Publishing.

Kabat-Zinn, J. (1994). *Wherever you go there you are: Mindfulness meditation in everyday life.* New York, NY: Hyperion.

Kegan, R. (1995). *In over our heads: The mental demands of modern life.* Cambridge, MA: Harvard University Press.

Laske, O. E. (2004). Looking for patterns in clients' developmental-behavioral dance with coaches. In I. Stein, F. Campone & L. J. Page (Eds.), *Proceedings of the Second ICF Coaching Research Symposium* (pp. 131-138). Washington, DC: International Coach Federation.

Laske, O. E., Stober, D., & Edwards, J. (2004). Whitepaper: What is, and why should we care about evidence-based coaching. In I. Stein, F. Campone & L. J. Page (Eds.), *Proceedings of the second ICF coaching research symposium* (pp. 169-173). Washington, DC: International Coach Federation.

Moustakas, C. (1990). *Heuristic research: Design, methodology, and applications.* Newbury Park, CA: Sage Publications.

Ñanamoli, N., & Bodhi, B. (Translator). (1995). *The middle length discourses of the Buddha: A new translation of the Majjhima Nik-aya.* Boston, MA: Wisdom Publications.

O'Neill, M. B. (2000). *Executive coaching with backbone and heart: A systems approach to engaging leaders with their challenges.* San Francisco, CA: Jossey-Bass.

Patton, Q. P. (1990). *Qualitative evaluation and research methods* (2nd ed.). Newbury Park, CA: Sage Publications.

Rahula, W. (1959). *What the Buddha taught.* New York, NY: Grove Weidenfeld.

Rubin, J. (1999, March). Close encounters of a new kind: Toward an integration of psychoanalysis and Buddhism. *American Journal of Psychoanalysis. Special Issue: Buddhism and psychoanalysis, 59*(1), 5-24.

Safran, J. (Ed.). (2003). *Psychoanalysis and Buddhism: An unfolding dialogue.* Boston, MA: Wisdom Publications.

Schein, E. (1992). *Organizational culture and leadership: A dynamic view* (2nd ed.). San Francisco, CA: Jossey-Bass.

Seligman, M. E. (2002). *Authentic happiness: Using the new positive psychology to realize your potential for lasting fulfillment.* New York, NY: Free Press.

Senge, P. (1990). *The fifth discipline: The art and practice of the learning organization.* New York, NY: Doubleday.

Sherman, S. & Freas, A. (2004, November). The wild west of executive coaching. *Harvard Business Review,* 82-90.

Torbert, B. (2004). *Action inquiry.* San Francisco, CA: Berrett-Koehler Publishers, Inc.

Witherspoon, R., & White, R. P. (1997). *Four essential ways that coaching can help executives.* Greensboro, NC: Center for Creative Leadership.

Barbara Braham, M.S.W., MCC is an executive and leadership coach, who works with management teams who want to move their organization forward and leaders who want to realize their potential. Her clients include executives in not-for-profits, government, higher education, associations and corporations.   Barbara is an author of eleven books including Finding Your Purpose and Be Your Own Coach (co-authored with Chris Wahl).

A student of the Dharma, she has had a daily vipassana meditation practice for the past 11 years. In addition to her daily practice she spends three to four weeks in silence each year. Her research interests include stages of adult development and spiritual practice, spiritual maturity in the Buddhist tradition, and the intersection of Buddhist practice and executive coaching. She earned a doctorate in interdisciplinary studies. Her dissertation was on executive coaching and vipassana meditation. Contact: barbara@bbraham.com.

Seeking Commonalities Amongst Evidence-Based Coaching Research: Observations of a Coach-Practitioner

Kerul Kassel

This paper presents the results of an interview study undertaken with ICF researchers to determine the current state of research on the effectiveness of coaching. The intent of the study was to distill common denominators in research studies of evidence-based coaching. Client self-reporting on a range of variables, as a measure of coaching effectiveness was the most frequent factor across research studies. Some self-reporting was quantitative, and much of it was more qualitative in nature.

Other recurring themes that emerged during the interviews centered on such professional issues as establishing coaching as a legitimate and respectable discipline. Concepts which were repeated across the board included (a) the need to construct a comprehensive theoretical foundation for coaching models and outcomes, (b) the need to educate new coaches in theory and scientifically researched processes, (c) the need for more process-oriented as well as evidence-based coaching research, and (d) the importance of enrolling coach-practitioners in becoming educated about current research and research methods.

In regard to the last issue, the author suggests that research findings be made more user-friendly for the larger coaching industry, both by composing secondary papers or articles that are more comprehensible to that audience, and by generating more visibility for findings through expanded avenues for publication of those articles.

Kerul Kassel is currently a senior faculty member at CoachVille. Her coaching company is New Leaf Systems. She is a Graduate of Coach U CTP and a CoachVille Certified graduate. She holds certification by both the ICF and the International Association of Coaches, and is a CoachVille Certified Mentor Coach and Certifier. Kerul holds a Master of Arts in Social Ecology from Goddard College. Contact: kerul@newleafsystems.com

The Effects of Executive Coaching on Self-Efficacy, Job Satisfaction, Organization Commitment, and Work/Family and Family/Work Conflict

Myra E. Dingman

The research question was, "How does the extent and quality of participation in an executive coaching relationship affect levels of self-efficacy, job satisfaction, organizational commitment, and the conflict between work and family?" The researcher defined executive coaching as a helping relationship between an executive with managerial authority and responsibility and a coach who utilizes the executive coaching process, combined with successful coaching behaviors and skills, to facilitate the executive's achievement of a mutually identified set of goals. These goals may include improving self-related and job-related outcomes. This study collected one-time survey data from 92 executives working in different organizations using (a) the new 18-item measure of the six-component executive coaching process (formal contracting, relationship building, assessment, getting feedback and reflecting, goal-setting, and implementation and evaluation) and (b) the 15-item measure of the quality of the coaching relationship (interpersonal skills, communication style, and instrumental support). Each participant was currently (or recently had been) in a coaching relationship with a coach trained in the Transformational Leadership Coaching program. The results indicated that the extent to which the six-component executive coaching process has been implemented in a coaching relationship had a positive relationship with higher job satisfaction. Brief (1998) concluded that job satisfaction and task performance have an elusive relationship; yet job satisfaction and contextual performance (individual contributions by employees to their work-place environment that supports task performance) have been found to be significantly related (Organ & Ryan, 1995). The second finding notes that the quality of the coaching relationship related to higher self-efficacy in the executives. This is a positive finding for organizations in that it may show that executives are looking for someone to connect with, and a coach provides this outlet. This may, in turn, lead to increased self-efficacy which is a central component of an employee's motivation and organizational performance (Bandura, 1997). Surprisingly, the quality of the coaching relationship had a negative relationship to job satisfaction. This may indicate that the stronger the coach's behaviors and skills are, the more likely they are to coach their client "out of their job" leading to lower job satisfaction.

References

Bandura, A. (1997). *Self-efficacy: The exercise of control.* New York, NY: Freeman.

Brief, A. P. (1998). *Attitudes in and around organizations.* Thousand Oaks, CA: Sage Publications, Inc.

Organ, D. W., & Ryan, K. (1995). A meta-analytic review of attitudinal and dispositional predictors of organizational citizenship behavior. *Personnel Psychology, 48*(4), 775-803.

Myra Dingman, Ph.D. has been a part of Regent University since 1998 where she is currently a Fellow with the Graduate School of Business. She became a certified coach in 2003, which led to her doctoral dissertation topic, "The Effects of Executive Coaching on Job-Related Attitudes." This executive coaching research was the first empirical study on the effects of executive coaching as a predictor of job satisfaction, organizational commitment, and work and family conflict of employees. It utilized the "Continuous Coaching Scale" that she developed. She earned her Ph.D. from the School of Leadership Studies at Regent University. Dr. Dingman is currently writing a leadership book and serving as an adjunct professor at Regent University. Contact myradin@regent.edu.

The Ten Dimensions Of Human Development: Toward a Unified Theory of Personal Growth

Hugh Martin
Kaye Martin

This presentation outlines a theory of human development, which synthesizes coaching, psychology, literature, science, and religion into all-embracing system for life improvement and personal evolution. Both theoretical and practical, this presentation is an invitation to focused inquiry and spirited discussion.

For coaching to progress, a set of unifying principles is essential. Two among the many potential benefits of such approaches stand out: cross-fertilization of knowledge and practical results. The proposed unified theory rests on ten major dimensions of human growth, listed below in order of increasing subtlety, complexity, and inclusiveness. The ten dimensions of personal development describe how a unified, integrated whole person can evolve to live a complete, balanced, harmonious whole life.

1. **The Self:** the center of our existence, the set of core identities that engage in life and grow in consciousness
2. **Biologic:** functions are the bodily organs and systems that sustain and empower life
3. **Habits:** our automatic responses and actions that become standardized and routine as a result of our training and conditioning
4. **Traits:** the fundamental building blocks of personality. These are the attributes and talents that distinguish us from other people
5. **Roles:** the character types formed by a unique combination of traits
6. **Arenas:** the twelve spheres of experience where daily living actually takes place. These include education, career, marriage, finances, and health
7. **Life Passages:** ten stages of life through which we all progress from infancy all the way through midlife and old age
8. **Self Passages:** the way we grow on the outside; the way we grow on the inside
9. **Soul passages:** the eight States of consciousness through which we can ascend as we shed the obsessions and compulsions of our material self.
10. **Processes:** the seven major procedures and techniques people use to facilitate growth in any of the ten dimensions; what makes growth actually happen

Hugh Martin is president of the NASD brokerage and advisory firm Hugh Martin & Co. He earned a BA degree from Swarthmore College, MA degree from University of Pennsylvania and completed doctoral studies at Indiana University. Contact: martinhugh@comcast.net.

Kaye Martin is a natural medicine practitioner and an instructor of nutrition and natural medicine at Baumann College. She is a life coach, natural food chef, and community organizer. She earned a BA degree from Cal State Northridge. Contact: martinakaye@comcast.net.

White paper 2005

Framing the Dialogue:
Unlocking Issues Surrounding Coaching Research

Linda J. Page
Irene F. Stein

Several questions raised during a panel discussion at the 2004 Second International Coach Federation (ICF) Coaching Research Symposium have continuing relevance for the profession and therefore deserve to be included in the dialogue. The authors summarize and expand on those questions, including the nature of coaching, what will be accepted as evidence, whether coaching will become a unique field of study, and how coach training can become coach education. They encourage an expansion of the dialogue beyond the Symposium and ICF itself to broaden and deepen the development of the field.

The theme of the Third ICF Coaching Research Symposium to be held November 2005, Coaching Research: Building Dialogue, highlights the importance of bringing voices from differing backgrounds and experiences together to frame the coaching-related research dialogue as broadly and deeply as possible. Truly, this dialogue has already been happening at and between the two previous ICF Coaching Research Symposia (Stein and Belsten, 2004; Stein, Campone, and Page, 2005) and will necessarily continue as the field of coaching studies moves forward in defining itself in conversation with a variety of other organizations and individuals.

This White paper highlights three main issues that were the focus of a panel discussion (Campone, Irwin, Hurd, Peterson, White, Page, and Bennett, 2004) at the Second ICF Coaching Research Symposium held in November 2004. In that panel, six coaches with various connections to research addressed a series of three questions under the title "Exploring Key Issues in Coaching Research."

Further consideration of the panel topics yields even more stimulus to ongoing dialogue, including questions about the nature of coaching itself. This paper will continue that conversation by bringing our (Linda's and Irene's) perspectives into the panelists' dialogue.

Question 1
What do we think evidence-based coaching means and what is its importance?

The term "evidence-based coaching" was first introduced to a wide audience by Anthony (Tony) M. Grant (2004), keynote speaker at the First ICF Coaching Research Symposium. Adapted from the term "evidence-based medicine" (Sackett, Haynes, Guyatt, and Tugwell, 1996), and reflected in research paradigms comfortable to those having a psychology background, entering "evidence-based coaching" into the lexicon of the coaching studies and professional coaching fields provides both a legitimizing and a limiting effect. At the very least, for those not from a medical or psychological background the term can be quite confusing.

Panelist Jean Hurd told of conducting an informal survey on what "evidence-based coaching" meant and discovering a good deal of confusion: "I heard everything from 'Evidence-based—that means quantitative research,' to 'No, it focuses on evidence that is based on practice, on what we experience in practice,' to 'Evidence-based coaching is a proprietary coaching methodology.'" In our experience, the term "evidence-based coaching" has been used to mean either strictly coaching from a theory and research basis, or alternatively, coaching from a reflective- or scientist-practitioner perspective—the former privileging formal knowledge and the latter privileging the coach's experience. Does "evidence-based coaching" mean that you have to know and ground your practice only in empirically tested coaching theory and research, or does it mean that a practitioner coaches by consciously testing his or her current practices, reflecting on results and adjusting practice accordingly?

In previous correspondence, Tony Grant reiterated his intended definition of evidence-based coaching, paralleling Sackett et al.'s (1996) explanation of evidence- based medicine, as "involving the intelligent and conscientious use of best current knowledge [from valid research theory and practice] in making decisions about how to design, implement and deliver coaching interventions to clients and in designing and teaching coach training programs" (Grant, 2004, p. 3). He added "from valid research and practice" in his definition since initial publication of his 2003 keynote paper in order to emphasize an expansive perspective of "knowledge" that includes both formal and experiential knowledge.

Panelist Jennifer Irwin added yet another dimension by explaining that evidence-based practice in her health care field has three components. It requires, in addition to the best currently available research evidence, the input of practitioner experience and insight, plus client preference. She suggested that confusion in using the term "evidence-based coaching" arises due to the multitude of academic fields that contribute to coaching: "The definition makes sense to me from my background in a health field, where evidence-based medicine is commonly accepted, but that's not the only field represented in coaching. We're probably thirty to fifty different fields coming together."

But what "best possible knowledge" is to be privileged in legitimizing coaching? What is to be accepted as "evidence" in a coaching context? Irwin suggests, "I don't think we are going to have a single answer to that because in some fields the best research is a rich in-depth qualitative study. In some fields, the best research is a randomized controlled trial. In other fields, it would be phenomenological approaches. In my opinion, we need to be open to all of the different approaches to research."

Thus, one task for future ICF Coaching Research Symposia and for coaching researchers in general is to clear up confusion regarding the model or models of evidence that will be acceptable in the field of coaching studies. In a previous whitepaper, Laske, Stober, and Edwards (2005) offered a "Definition of Evidence Relevant to Coach Training and Coaching Practice":

> Empirical evidence is typically not something that is simply "found." Rather, it is constructed, and it derives from theoretical models that determine the perspective and interpretive analysis of findings.... Understanding and interpreting such evidence requires knowledge of research techniques and their methodological limits (p. 170-171).

In her keynote address, Dianne Stober (2005) recommended drawing upon the "scientist-practitioner" model from the field of psychology as a guide for coaching researchers. Panelist Linda Page questioned whether coaching would be served by models such as manualized psychotherapy research. The question remains of which existing fields provide theoretical models that most effectively "determine the perspective and interpretive analysis of findings" and therefore ground the construction of empirical studies in coaching.

Thinking more broadly, to what extent should coaching develop its own models, building on but not limited to existing fields of study? Answering this question demands a thorough knowledge of scholarly and research history, but also an openness to the demands of twenty-first century scholarship. Is coaching, or could it be, a truly new field of study, or is it simply a revised application of existing theories and research? Coaches may do well to think of this potentially new field of study as one that can contribute to the wider world of theory and research, not just to borrow and take guidance from it.

Speaking to a more specific issue, Hurd pointed out during the panel that much of the drive toward evidence-based coaching is a "striving for legitimacy." But, she suggested, the assumption that integrating research into coaching practice will produce more effective coaches has not itself been tested by research. "We don't actually have the studies, the evidence, which says we will get that result....It is commendable to want to use evidence when we are working with a client. But we really don't know how to do that yet—how to read it, how to interpret it, and whether we are causing any harm."

As a contribution to the question of whether research will enhance practice, panelist David Peterson reported that coaches generally have evidence that what they do works. "But I think that standard is too low. Rather than, 'Does it work?' the question should be, 'Are there other approaches that are better? What's the most effective choice to make for this particular person that I'm working with right now, given what they need?' That's where I think we have a huge lack of evidence. I'm sure that coaching as done by most coaches is just fine. But that's too low a hurdle. 'What works best?' When we can answer that, we will really become a profession." This ongoing reflective practice is what Page (2005) referred to as "expertising," or the process of developing mastery.

In summary, though the use of the term "evidence-based coaching" has been easily misunderstood and still does have the potential to limit what "legitimate" means in coaching practices, we believe that 'the horse has left the barn' and that the use of the term is firmly entrenched in the coaching studies lexicon. The specific question of whether coaching should adopt an evidence-based standard leads to as yet unanswered questions of what "evidence" means in the context of coaching, and of what coaching is as a field of study that anchors the practice of coaching. We advocate a realization that coaching, and therefore coaching studies, is an emerging new species that draws on but is not limited to inherited knowledge or a variant that represents a temporary reshuffling of existing approaches.

More specifically, coaching researchers are challenged to provide evidence that "evidence-based coaching" will enhance practice and further will yield an understanding of what works best. We agree with panelists Hurd and Irwin who say we should be broad and inclusive in what we consider evidence. And we agree with Stober's (personal correspondence, 2005) definition for "evidence-based coaching," also informed by Sackett et al. (1996), as encompassing what she thinks most of us see as essential requirements for effective intervention: (a) the use of the best available knowledge; integrated with (b) the coach's expertise; and applied to (c) the particular client's context, preferences, and culture. This is the definition we should move forward with as the field of coaching studies is defined.

Question 2:
What are the motivations for coaching research? And how should we regard them?

Certainly, "legitimacy" in the eyes of other fields, such as psychology and healthcare, would be enhanced through the dissemination of rigorously conducted coaching research. But also, as panelist Katharine White points out, increasingly savvy potential customers are looking for concrete evidence that coaching is effective. It's not enough for coaches just to say, "My clients seem to be happy, so I must be effective." Panelists White and Peterson further dissected the question of motivation for coaching research. Here we both present and comment on their astute observations and extend the consequences of their answer to a broader dialogue on issues of coaching research.

Panelist Peterson gave a twist to this question by considering reasons for not doing research: first, doing good research is difficult; second, it is expensive; third, it challenges our cherished beliefs. All great points, but if the reasons Peterson and White offer for doing research (see below) are convincing, then these three challenges must be overcome. Indeed, overcoming these challenges will shape the nature of how the coaching studies field views research and how it will organize itself.

In response to the first challenge, the difficulty of doing good research, coaches who wish to conduct research must be trained to do so, or scholars who already have those skills must be recruited. There must be educational resources to introduce already-trained scholars to the context and content of coaching. In both cases, where and how will this training occur? The question of training is discussed more fully below.

The second challenge, the expense in time and money for conducting coaching research, brings up questions of what kind of research will be done. It is possible in certain contexts, especially in organizational coaching, to build funding for evaluation (including return-on-investment—ROI) into the cost of coaching. But to really get at ROI, research needs to be done in defining coaching itself and in operationalizing coaching outcomes. Research into more basic questions, such as why something works, is not as easy to justify as part of the provision of organizational coaching. Typically, basic research is done in university departments for the very reason that they have the resources. However, with the current scarcity of funded "coaching studies" departments, basic coaching research is being done by faculty and graduate students in other academic departments, based on the theoretical models of those academic fields. Those, mostly traditional, models will "determine the perspective and interpretive analysis of findings" (Laske et al., 2005, p. 170). Are these models the best fit for studying non-traditional aspects of coaching? Where, then, will the opportunity for a uniquely coaching field of study arise?

Regarding the third challenge to research, the attitude behind the research enterprise in general is a skeptical one, one that questions exactly the beliefs that individuals, organizations or fields of study cherish most strongly. As panelist Page put it, "Every one of us operates out of a set of assumptions, and assumption is another word for unexamined theory. To move forward as an emerging profession, we have to become aware of the theories that guide us, and then we can devise research to test those theories."

Will coaching become a profession? If coaches are so wedded to their assumptions about coaching and how it works that they are unwilling to subject those unexamined theories to testing, then coaching is more like a cult or a marketing brand where the important questions are how to exclude, ignore, or put a spin on potentially embarrassing enquiry. Laske et al. (2005) issued a call to action to bring about a second phase in the evolution of coaching, one that establishes coaching as a field of study rather than only a marketing brand. Whether coaching answers that call is being decided at events such as the ICF Coaching Research Symposia and other venues.

Panelists Peterson and White offered eight motivations for coaching research:

- To satisfy curiosity.
- To answer specific questions.
- To improve coaching processes.
- To enhance decision making.
- To sharpen marketing.
- To design new tools and techniques.
- To ground the training of new coaches.
- To grow the profession of coaching.

White added, "We don't all have to be researchers doing research on our practice, but we all have to find ways to incorporate research into our practice. We can't think that we can bypass this step when no other emerging profession bypassed it and lived to tell the tale."

In summary, overcoming obstacles to doing research requires individual practitioner decisions to learn about and include evidence regarding successful outcome. But to delve more deeply into basic research questions leads again to the more general question of whether coaching will become a unique field of study or will leave basic research to already-existing fields located in university departments—each with its own paradigm that may not capture all the possibilities that a coaching field could explore. Moving in the direction of a coaching field of study means opening all of coaching's cherished "truths" to research. That is, accepting a much more questioning, skeptical attitude, one that is not driven primarily by marketing considerations.

Question 3:
How can coaching research be brought into the preparation and education of coaches?

Panelists Page and John Bennett drew a distinction between "coach training" and "coach education." As is typical in scholar-practitioner fields, a field of coaching studies would necessarily incorporate research, theory, and practice. Coach training emphasizes the practice aspect and concentrates on teaching skills, while coach education would have a higher emphasis on theory and research, which go hand-in-hand. An overarching paradigm in which to situate coaching research, theory and practice may involve specifically highlighting the interplay between the three. Stober's keynote address (Stober, 2005) about coaches as scientist-practitioners seemed to support this type of paradigm.

More specific consideration of the role of trainers and educators was discussed by panelist Page when she asserted that coach training, very little of which currently involves research and theory, is more limited than coach education. "Professional education recognizes the interdependence of theory, research, and practice…Coach training organizations must not only develop a more educational orientation, but also engage in a series of conversations with emerging coach educators in academic departments so as to both forge the future and maintain the heritage of coaching."

Panelist Bennett suggested that not every trained coach needs to be conversant in theory and research and presented a three-level model, with the largest level at the base of a triangle being the practitioner. "While practitioners need to have a grounding in what theory is at play in the training they receive, they may not need to understand it at great depth and detail. There is a middle group that we would call the scholar-practitioner. This is the person who is engaged in the practice of coaching but who is also engaged in the conversation about theory and testing theory and doing research. And then there may be a small group of people whose interest is almost exclusively that of scholars developing a field of coaching."

We believe that the addition of "skills to be a reflective practitioner" to the ICF list of coaching competencies would help to shift the focus of all coaching practitioners at least a bit toward the "scientist-practitioner" stance that Stober (2005) advocates. To this end, panelist White recommended linking the levels of certification to "…an improving ability to think critically, to test theories, to look at outcomes." She suggested that such a linkage would enhance the credibility of ICF's certification process, as there is a question whether simply more hours of coaching necessarily means one is getting better at it. As panelist Page pointed out, research in expertise (Bereiter and Scardamalia, 1993) indicates that practice may be necessary for mastery, but practice alone is not sufficient. "It takes about 10,000 hours of practice in most fields in order to develop mastery. But you can practice for 10,000 hours and not be an expert. Witness my cooking," said Page. "How practice, training, and education are best combined in the preparation of coaches is a question that is open to research."

Laske et al. (2005) wondered whether the development of evidence-based coaching programs in universities will overwhelm existing proprietary coach training organizations run on a business model. "But," they wrote, "it is certain that the next several years will be a period of shakeout in determining what is perceived as valid training and acceptable expertise in coaching."

The Second ICF Coaching Research Symposium, for all its success, revealed a glaring gap: the coach trainers and educators, the people who provide the skeletal foundation for coaches, were not as prominently a part of that 2004 Symposium as would be necessary if research is to become fully and permanently integrated into the coaching body.

Surely, if the existing training schools are to participate in the development and maintenance of a field of coaching studies, they should be involved in events such as the ICF Coaching Research Symposia.

In order to promote greater participation by coaching trainers and educators in Third ICF Coaching Research Symposium, the Board of Directors of the Association of Coach Training Organizations offered to co-sponsor a part of the program at the Third ICF Coaching Research Symposium. As a result, this 2005 Symposium has the opportunity to engage trainers and educators in the research conversation along with the researchers and practitioners who were involved in previous Symposia.

In summary, we, along with ACTO, see the necessity of including coach training organizations and academic coaching programs in the discussion of the future of coaching education and research. Doing so will expand the concept of coach training to include a broader definition of coach education and may enable the certification process to become more of a measure of mastery. These steps are part of a developmental shift in coaching with the potential to result in a profession that is more grounded in theory and research.

Coaching Research: Whither and How?

We draw several conclusions from the 2004 panel discussion and the ongoing dialogue that both informed and was stimulated by it. First, we recognize that the term "evidence-based coaching" is here to stay, with the promise of providing guiding principles for coaching practice and training, as well as research. That promise will be fulfilled so long as, the definition of "evidence" as used in coaching theory and applied to coaching research and practice matches the unique needs and characteristics of coaching, rather than definitions from other fields. "Evidence" should be defined broadly, including many kinds of empirical, as well as intuitive, knowledge. "Evidence-based coaching," then, would be a coaching intervention that integrates the best current knowledge from theory and research, with the reflective practitioner's expertise, and the client's context and preferences.

Second, the needs and characteristics of coaching will be spelled out through the development of a unique field of coaching studies, which will provide a nexus for ongoing coaching theory and research development as well as a necessary foundation for the professional practice of coaching. This field may draw on theory and research from existing fields such as developmental psychology, adult education, human resources management, organizational development, consulting, health and wellness, counseling and psychotherapy, communication, and others. But it should neither be limited to, nor dependent solely on, any current academic field or discipline. Indeed, with the unique way that coaches see the world, a field of coaching studies has the potential to develop research methods and a foundational paradigm that contributes to new ways of approaching the social sciences. As a practical outcome of this process, we expect to see the emergence of even more university departments of coaching studies (see Williams, 2005), making further resources available to stimulate and disseminate coaching research.

Third, the call to overcome the obstacles to coaching research and to embrace its promise is being answered far beyond ICF and its series of Coaching Research Symposia: by ICF regional conferences in Europe and Australia; Professional Coaches and Mentors

Association conferences; the International Consortium for Coaching in Organizations; First and Second Conferences on Evidence-Based Coaching sponsored by the Coaching Psychology Unit at the University of Sydney; and sessions at psychology, counseling, human resources, training and development, consulting, and management conferences. In addition to specific journals dedicated to coaching, such as the International Journal of Coaching in Organizations and the International Journal of Evidence Based Coaching and Mentoring, coaching-related articles have appeared in the Journal of Consulting Psychology: Research and Practice, the Journal of Individual Psychology, journals of the Academy of Management, and others. The job of tracking, providing access to, and integrating these strands of research and theory will be a major challenge for the new field of coaching studies—and will provide a foundation for it.

Fourth, a narrowly-defined "scientist-practitioner" model borrowed from clinical psychology may provide a guide for those coaching researchers who dedicate a substantial portion of their time to research and theory development. However, for the majority of practitioners, the scientist-practitioner model should be interpreted broadly as a reminder of the importance of reflecting on one's own practice, of seeking out and interpreting evidence that can improve that practice, and of participating in research wherever and whenever possible. Thus, the term "reflective practitioner" or "scholar-practitioner" may be more suitable for the majority of coaching practitioners, and should represent a required skill for the professional coach.

Fifth, we conceive of a two-pronged approach to stimulating the emergence of a coaching field of studies, the expansion of coaching research and the integration of evidence into coaching practice. One prong is the incorporation of theory and research into coach training, which will transform it into coach education. This process is under way in existing coach training schools, as evidenced by ACTO's participation in the Third ICF Coaching Research Symposium in 2005, and in coaching programs at professional schools and accredited universities such as the University of Sydney, Georgetown University, Royal Roads University, the University of Texas at Dallas, Fielding Graduate University, and others. The second prong would be the linking of training school accreditation and individual coach certification to the development of reflective practitioner skills.

Finally, while we applaud the increasing visibility of coaching research since the First ICF Coaching Research Symposium, including the growth in submissions and attendance at the Second ICF Coaching Research Symposium and incorporation of research into regular sessions at various ICF-sponsored and other coaching conferences, we believe some further steps are necessary to ensure that coaching research continues to grow in both quantity and quality. A single day Coaching Research Symposium as an ICF pre-conference event gives insufficient time to have the research discussion necessary to meet the challenges outlined above. It is also increasingly difficult in one event to meet the needs and adjust the terminology of discussion for diverse audience participants that consist of practitioners wanting to learn about research, coach training school representatives wanting to improve their schools' offerings, scholars studying, developing and teaching coach theory, and finally active and potential researchers. Besides planning the program, considerable work is required for the single day of the ICF Coaching Research Symposium: calling for papers, conducting a peer-review, and producing a compendium of the papers as the symposium proceedings.

As the numbers of researchers and research papers increase, and more technical questions of methodology arise, it may be useful to plan a two- or three-day conference dedicated to more basic research presentations. Such a scholar- and researcher-oriented conference would be the forum for a mostly academic treatment of coach theory and research. The resulting information from that conference could feed into a separate, more practitioner- or trainer-oriented, event associated with the ICF Annual Conference at a later date. Perhaps such a conference should be sponsored by an organization that has as its sole purpose to encourage research and the skeptical attitudes that go with it, rather than one oriented to protecting the interests of its members. This conference, and perhaps such an organization, could be a center for an academic treatment of coaching studies—producing a conference, conducting informational forums, and producing publications such as a peer-reviewed Journal of Coaching Studies.

It is a characteristic of change in complex systems that individual points of creativity are distributed widely throughout the system. Coaching, taken as a worldwide phenomenon, is indeed a varied and complex system, and it is clear that the system is undergoing change. Therefore, our suggestions are surely matched by others, probably by dozens or even hundreds of others. Each such point of creativity can contribute to the emergence of coaching as a profession by attempting to link and glean best ideas from the others. Informed by discussion from the "Key Issues in Coaching Research" panel at the Second ICF Coaching Research Symposium (Campone et al., 2004), this whitepaper is itself a point in the ongoing dialogue, adding our voice to the wisdom of our many colleagues. We look forward to a further exchange of ideas at the Third ICF Coaching Research Symposium, and we encourage as wide a continuing dialogue as possible in the future. The directions we go and the actions we take in developing a field of coaching studies to house coaching-related theory, research and practice will necessarily emerge from that broadly held dialogue.

Reference

Bereiter, C. & Scardamalia, M. (1993). Surpassing ourselves: an inquiry into the nature and implications of expertise. Chicago, IL: Open Court.

Campone, F. (Chair), Irwin, J., Hurd, J., Peterson, D., White, K., Page, L. J., & Bennett, J. L. (2004, November). Key issues in coaching research. Panel conducted at The Second Annual ICF Research Symposium, Quebec, Canada. Audiotape available from www.audiotape.com, Product Code IF04RS2.

Grant, A. M. (2004). Keeping up with the Cheese! Research as a foundation for professional coaching of the future. In I. F. Stein & L. A. Belsten (Eds.), *Proceedings of the First ICF Coaching Research Symposium* (pp. 1-19). Mooresville, NC: Paw Print Press.

Laske, O. E., Stober, D. R., & Edwards, J. (2005). Whitepaper: What is, and why should we care about, evidence-based coaching? In I. F. Stein, F. Campone & L. J. Page (Eds.), *Proceedings of the Second ICF Coaching Research Symposium* (pp. 169-174). Washington, DC: International Coach Federation.

Page, L. J. (2005). Research as "expertising": A reading guide for practicing coaches. In I. F. Stein & F. Campone & L. J. Page (Eds.), *Proceedings of the Second ICF Coaching Research Symposium* (pp. 146-153). Washington, DC: International Coach Federation.

Sackett, D. L., Haynes, R. B., Guyatt, G. H., & Tugwell, P. (1996). Evidence based medicine: What it is and what it isn't. *British Medical Journal, 312*(7023), 71-72.

Stein, I. F., & Belsten, L. A. (Eds.). (2004). *Proceedings of the First ICF Coaching Research Symposium.* Mooresville, NC: Paw Print Press.

Stein, I. F., Campone, F., & Page, L. J. (Eds.). (2005). *Proceedings of the Second ICF Coaching esearch Symposium.* Washington, DC: International Coach Federation.

Stober, D. R. (2005). Coaching eye for the research guy and research eye for the coaching guy: 20/20 vision for coaching through the scientist-practitioner model. In I. F. Stein & F. Campone & L. J. Page (Eds.), *Proceedings of the Second ICF Coaching Research Symposium* (pp. 13-21). Washington, DC: International Coach Federation.

Williams, P. (2005, August). Graduate coaching degrees: How will they affect the profession? Academic institutions enter the coach training arena. In B. Barry (Ed.), *Coaching World,* e-newsletter of International Coach Federation, http://www.coach-federation.org/newsletter/currentIssue.htm. Accessed 29, August, 2005.

An edited transcript may be obtained from the authors, Linda J. Page or Irene F. Stein.

Linda J. Page, Ph.D., M.A., ACPC is founder and president of the Adler School of Professional Coaching Inc. She taught communications, sociology, anthropology, science and human affairs, history and philosophy of science, psychology, and technical writing at colleges and universities in the United States and Canada. She completed an M.A. in Counseling Psychology from the Adler School of Professional Psychology (ASPP) and founded the Psychotherapy Institute of Toronto in 1987. She earned a doctorate degree in Sociology and Anthropology from Princeton University where she did research in sociolinguistics. She is a Licensed Clinical Professional Counselor in the State of Illinois and was a member of the doctoral core faculty at ASPP in Chicago from 1992 to 1998 where she supervised a number of doctoral dissertations. She became an Adler Certified Professional Coach in 2002. Contact: ljpage@adler.ca.

Irene F. Stein, ACC is currently enrolled in the doctoral program in Human and Organizational Systems at Fielding Graduate University. She combines her academic studies with her professional coaching experience to research and development of coaching theories and practices. Irene was the Lead Organizer and editor of the Proceedings of the First International Coach Federation (ICF) Coaching Research Symposium and was Co-Leader and co-editor of the Proceedings of the Second ICF Coaching Research Symposium. He earned the Accredited Certified Coach (ACC) credential through the ICF. Contact: irenestein@att.net.

White paper 2005

Riding The Waves:
A Quantum Framework for
Coaching-related Research

Francine Campone

> *As the variety of papers in this Proceedings and the two which preceded it show, we conduct coaching-related research for a wide variety of reasons and in many different ways. The questions we choose to explore, the methods we use to collect information and the way we go about making sense of what we collect are all informed by our academic and professional experiences as well as by our personal values and perspectives. Coaching researchers draw on the literature and methodologies of several disciplines and professional practices. Our research also reflects what we believe the purposes of coaching to be: a means of encouraging individual growth, organizational development and, for some, social change. Given the multifaceted nature of coaching-related research, the task of facilitating a review process for this Research Symposium has offered many learning opportunities. In this paper, I summarize some of the thinking and learning which resulted. In addition, I suggest a framework for coaching-related research, which could credibly advance the development of coaching as professional practice.*

The Many Faces of Coaching Research

In recent years, I have participated in the paper review and co-editing processes for the International Coach Federation (ICF) Research Symposium and Proceedings. The papers, which have been presented, coupled with the keynote addresses (Grant, 2004; Stober, 2005) and White paper (Laske, Stober, and Edwards, 2005), represent a variety of research paradigms. These encompass pure qualitative designs (Severin, 2004), mixed qualitative-quantitative designs (Lew, Wolfred, Gibson and Con, 2004; McCready 2005), and an array of qualitative designs including Appreciative Inquiry (Bush, 2005), narrative analysis (Drake, 2005); hermeneutic phenomenology (Hurd, 2004) and grounded theory (Edwards, 2005). Beyond the ICF Research Symposiums and Proceedings, *The International Journal of Coaching in Organizations* issue on coaching research ((Bush & Lazar, 2005) showed a similar spectrum of interests and methods. Overall, studies in coaching implicitly or explicitly are rooted in a real world research orientation. This recognizes that coaching itself is, in its present state, an art rather than a science; that coaching interactions take place in an open system and are therefore subject to various undefined and perhaps unknowable conditions; and that, without a foundational literature, the coaching community lacks a shared language for framing, interpreting and presenting such inquiries.

The absence of shared language presented an early challenge in the preparation of this paper: how to best refer to the topic under consideration. The majority of sources cited use the term coaching research (Grant, 2004; Stober, 2005; Laske et al. 2005). Bennett (in press) uses the term coaching-related research and presents six themes found within such research: the coach, the client, the coach-client relationship, the process of coaching, the results of coaching, and the theories related to the practice and teaching of coaching. In effect, the term coaching-related research defines the research themes, which promote the development of coaching as a profession. On reflection, I view the term coaching research as broad, encompassing studies about coaching (for example, a demographic profile of practicing coaches), as well as studies in coaching. For purposes of this paper, I have adopted Bennett's term, coaching-related research, to position the proposed framework as most relevant to studies addressing his identified themes.

The purposes for which coaching-related research is undertaken are as diverse as coaches themselves. In a study of coaching researchers (Campone, unpublished manuscript), respondents offered motivations which included pragmatism and intellectual curiosity in almost equal measure. Practical motives included meeting requirements for doctoral degrees, documenting outcomes of organizational coaching, and creating coaching algorithms for purposes of standardizing programs. Intellectually curious coaches who conduct research want to better understand the underlying dynamics of coaching and to provide a solid basis for improving their coaching practices. Most of the respondents also stated that they and their coaching changed as the result of their intimate engagement with the data and the research process. While two-thirds drew on their academic backgrounds, many also used such skills as project management, interviewing and information mapping which they had honed in the course of their professional practice. Thus, the skill sets, which underpin coaching-related research, include traditional academic research methods and hands-on practical experience. This pattern of engagement between coach-researcher and the research process itself is akin to the model of reflective practitioner advocated by Schön (1983), who stated that reflection in action "tends to focus interactively on the outcomes of the action, the action itself and the intuitive knowing implicit in the action" (p.56). The subjective elements of coaching-related research appear to be integral to the field itself.

The emergent nature of the coaching field, coupled with the even more nascent status of coaching research, offers fertile ground for integrative, iterative research strategies. The variations of terms, assumptions, methodologies and standards reflected in current coaching-related research echo the current state of research practices in a variety of human disciplines including psychology, sociology, anthropology and education. Constructing an integrative perspective on coaching-related research brings a number of lenses into play. These include traditional quantitative research paradigms complemented, supplemented or replaced by a new landscape of qualitative research, the topography of which includes constructivist, interpretive, and hermeneutic perspectives and diverse critical theories, with a concomitant complex of norms, standards and paradigms (Denzin and Lincoln, 2003).

Entering the Stream

Irene Stein (2004) proposed that the Symposium Proceedings would serve as a platform for members of the coaching research community. She also expressed the hope that the coaching research community would "keep setting higher standards for ourselves in terms of rigorousness of thought, clarity of writing and careful planning, conducting and presentation of research" (p. xi). Given the fluid and ever-broadening landscape of research design, my colleague John Bennett and I devised a set of guidelines for the volunteer reviewers that we hoped would allow a fair and inclusive review process for the researchers and a learning process for ourselves. Our intention was to provide a set of review criteria, which were broad enough to apply to diverse research paradigms yet appropriately academic and professional. The guidelines reflected what, in our experience, are academic values: clear writing, original thinking, a contribution to advancing the profession, appropriate methodology and presentation of data, and sufficient references to the literature to ground the paper. Each paper was reviewed by two individuals and, if their recommendations diverged, was referred to a third reviewer.

Reviewer responses included a rating on each criterion, recommendation comments, and feedback for the authors. Reviewers were asked about their preference for reviewing quantitative or qualitative papers and wherever possible we honored those. Papers that were not recommended earned that status for reasons other than paradigmatic disagreement. None of the reviewers' feedback reflected deeply held convictions about a right way and a wrong way to do research. In some instances, the reviewer comments pointed the authors toward other resources, models or ideas, which were incorporated into their revised papers.

My learning started to emerge in a rereading of the reviewer feedback once all the logistics of sending the outcomes and feedback to authors had been addressed and revised papers were returned. The reviewers' application of the guidelines, coupled with concepts in the literature on research, suggested a framework for following Irene's injunction to "keep setting higher standards…" and provide a platform for all who have a contribution to the coaching field. The learning, presented below, is offered as a starting point for establishing a framework, which could inform subsequent coaching-related research symposiums and serve as one piece of the foundation establishing coaching as a professional field.

A Quantum Framework for Coaching-Related Research

Physicist Werner Heisenberg and his peers upended the paradigm of Newtonian science by introducing the Uncertainty Principle. 1 This set up a relationship between the observer and the observed by introducing the element of the observer's choice of where and how to focus. It also effected a significant shift in the practice of science by demonstrating that the act of observation changes what's being observed. What does this have to do with the way we view coaching-related research? By offering reviewers a framework that would allow a spectrum of possible research paradigms, the review process functioned reasonably well with an acceptable degree of uncertainty. Taking that concept a step further, a shared framework for coaching-related research could help focus discussion within the coaching research community and, with refinements and revisions, stand as an espoused theory of coaching-related research to be tested in action. Robson (2002) notes the perception of an ideological divide in social science research overall and states that, in his own view, "many of these differences are more apparent and real and that there can be advantages in combining qualitative and quantitative approaches" (p.6). To do so, he recommends a "promiscuous approach" to real world research while underscoring the critical elements of rigor and rules or principles of procedure.

Heisenberg's demonstration of the Uncertainty Principle and related quantum principles was preceded by centuries of foundational research in Physics. Thus physicists had a body of foundational literature and a shared language- mathematics- with which to represent those ideas in theory-building. The field of coaching and coaching-related research is simultaneously seeking to document and verify the foundational principles and advance developing models and theories. While the dialogue urged by Barnett Pearce (in press) and facilitated in the 2005 Symposium program will undoubtedly contribute to mutual understanding and the development of accepted frameworks and theories of coaching, the praxis of coaching-related research is in need of a paradigm of its own. Building on the concepts we applied in the 2005 review process, I propose six principles which, taken together, might serve as a framework to guide the practice of coaching-related research. Each principle allows the possibility for any coaching-related research undertaking to emerge as a singular and bounded research event (akin to Heisenberg's particle) and as an element of an increasing flow- the wave of coaching-related research.

Principle One

Coaching-related research proceeds from real world coaching experiences, practices or parameters and seeks to answer a valid question. In considering the antecedents of successful research, Robson (2002) identifies five key elements:

- Activity and involvement, both within the field of practice and within the professional community of practice
- Convergence of two or more activities, interests and opportunities
- Intuition about timing and the "rightness" of the work
- Concern for theoretical understanding
- Real world value deriving from the exploration of questions arising within practice and resulting in "tangible and useful ideas."

Applying these to coaching-related research, this principle suggests the focus of inquiry is not purely speculative and that the questions, which are explored, are in some way answerable. Valid questions may seek to address gaps in the knowledge base of the field, shed new light on the researcher's work or nuances of practice, or raise issues and produce critiques (Chenail, 2003). The principle further suggests the researcher's interests, research posture and chosen methods are aligned and the researcher proceeds as a "curious investigator".

Principle Two

Coaching-related research respects and honors the integrity, autonomy and privacy of clients, coaches and the coaching relationship. Crawshaw's (in press) exposition of the ethical issues within coaching-related research is relevant regardless of the research paradigm followed. At present procedures ensuring the integrity and transparency of person and process appear to be a concern mainly for coaches pursuing doctoral research and for academics writing for professional publication. For doctoral students, a university's review board oversees the process and ensures compliance with the appropriate codes of conduct adhered to by credentialed professionals. As coaching-related research increasingly takes place apart from the academic setting, issues of integrity will carry greater weight. As with all of these principles, there are implications for the training and education of coaches in the principles and practices of coaching-related research. The key element of this principle is ensuring that a coach researcher maintains transparency with all study participants on matters of confidentiality, the purposes, uses and processes of the study, the implications of study participation and freedom of choice. In keeping with this principle, consent is as likely to be an iterative and on-going process as it is a one-time matter.

Principle Three

Coaching-related research is a purposeful inquiry, which contributes to the fundamentals of the coaching field (coaching and coach education theories, practices and principles) and to the coach researcher's professional growth and evolution. Whereas the first principle addresses the questions raised in coaching-related research, this principle suggests the purposes of such research. This principle integrates elements of the scientist-practitioner model referred to in keynote addresses at previous ICF Research Symposiums (Grant, 2004; Stober, 2005) and the reflective practitioner model (Schön, 1983). Given the field of coaching is simultaneously developing a foundational literature and norms and standards for professional practice (and by implication for preparing practitioners), it seems appropriate to encourage research which can address multiple purposes. A coaching-focused revision of scientist-practitioner research purposes might include (a) to develop a better understanding of the human change process; (b) to improve the accuracy and reliability of coaching assessment and outcomes measures; (c) to develop more grounded methods of coaching interventions; (d) to develop more grounded models for promoting client change and growth. The research questions may be driven by the coach researcher's individual interests or by the interests of some external organization. Alternatively, research questions may emerge as a result of constructed, collective thinking within the coaching-related research community.

Principle Four

Coaching-related research follows and makes transparent systematic methods of information gathering and analysis. We don't want to find ourselves in the position of the two scientists depicted in a cartoon given to me by a colleague years ago. Both fellows, wearing lab coats, are standing in front of a chalkboard containing a lengthy equation, the mathematical symbols of which are interrupted at mid-point by the phrase "and then a miracle happens." One scientist is telling the other "I think you need to do a little more work on step two." Whatever research paradigm a coach researcher proceeds from, the inquiry process must follow the protocols directed by academic convention. For example, following an interactive model of research design (Maxwell, 2005), a rigorous process of information gathering and analysis begins with specifying the goals of the study and a conceptual framework. These in turn influence the formulation of research questions, selection of methodologies and strategies to ensure validity. In writing up the study, the researcher includes the concepts, variables, relevant factors and the ideas, beliefs, and assumptions, which inform the study. As we learn together to strengthen coaching-related research, we need to show the thinking behind the thinking and the material on which the thinking focuses. Transparency in research methods ensures the credibility of the resulting study.

Principle Five

Coaching-related research promotes a scholarly integration of coaching theory and practice. Theories, methods and practices of coaching draw upon disparate fields. Coaches offer clients reflections, which integrate their speaking and implicit thinking, coach observations and external data. Similarly, coaching-related research can weave together the threads of actions- both the participants' and the researcher's- with underlying theories drawn from the coach's own experiences coupled with the external data of literature. Returning for a moment to Heisenberg, this principle suggests that each study in coaching acknowledges all of the potential states, or uses, to which the study can be put:

> "…as information to deepen individual coaching practice, as a building block in the creation of a foundational literature for a field and as a model for subsequent coaching-related research."

Principle Six

Coaching-related research presents enough artifacts (quantitative data, texts, descriptions, researcher reflections) to enable others to share the researcher's understanding. As noted earlier, coaching-related research can serve several purposes. As we contribute to the field's knowledge base, the studies we undertake must meet tests of validity. Valid studies, regardless of the research paradigm used, provide sufficient documentation to support credibility in descriptions, conclusions, explanations and interpretations. They contain the possibility of testing by others. The researcher recognizes the ways that these might be wrong and makes clear the strategies used to rule out threats (Robson, 2002). In quantitative research, these may include various controls in sampling; formulation of hypotheses; ensuring the integrity of the data and data collection; and the manipulation of statistical processes to exclude extraneous variables. In qualitative research, questions of validity need to be addressed before, during and after the research process. Maxwell (2005) identifies several strategies, which may be applied to acknowledge specific threats within a given study. These include long-term and intensive involvement of the researcher in the phenomenon being explored; ensuring that the data are rich, detailed and varied enough to provide a full picture; systematically soliciting respondent validation and feedback about the data and conclusions; seeking and investigating discrepant evidence and negative cases; triangulation; and comparisons of data across time, events or between actual and theoretical examples.

Conclusions

To grow the field of coaching as a profession, it is necessary to develop a framework for coaching-related research. Such a shared framework would accomplish several purposes: a) to establish the credibility of the theories, models and outcome studies which are presented as the foundational literature of the coaching field; b) to establish norms and standards which can be integrated into the education and training of coaches, enabling them to be informed consumers of research; c) to create a shared language and norms for the coaching-related research community. I do not expect that coaching researchers, or for that matter our colleagues in related fields, will come to certainty or consensus any time soon about a universally agreed upon research paradigm. The proposed principles and the framework they form are intended to open a dialogue and to suggest some elements, which warrant considerable exploration, refinement and testing. Our laboratory is real life. Coaching helps people break through to new paradigms of life and leadership. A quantum framework for coaching-related research will enable us, as a community of practitioners, to break through to new paradigms of meaningful inquiry within and about the work that we do.

References

Bennett, J. L. (in press). An agenda for coaching-related research: A challenge for researchers. *Journal of Consulting Psychology: Research and Practice.*

Bush, M.W. (2005). Client perceptions of effectiveness in executive coaching. In I. F. Stein, F. Campone, & L. J. Page (Eds.), *Proceedings of the Second International Coaching Federation Coaching Research Symposium* (pp. 30-37). Washington, DC: International Coach Federation.

Bush, M. W. & Lazar, J. (Eds.). *The International Journal of Coaching in Organization. 3*(1).

Campone, F. A well-informed curiosity: Evolving a model of coaching research. Unpublished manuscript.

Chenail, R. J. (2000). Navigating the "Seven C's": Curiosity, confirmation, comparison, changing, collaborating, critiquing and combination. The Qualitative Report. 4, March 2000. Retrieved January 6, 2005 from http://www.nova.edu/ssss/QR/QR4-3/sevencs.htm.

Crawshaw, L. (in press). Ethical considerations in qualitative coaching research. In F. Campone & J. L. Bennett (Eds.), *Proceedings of the Third International Coaching Federation Coaching Research Symposium.* Lexington, KY: International Coach Federation.

Denzin, N. K, & Lincoln, Y. S. (Eds.). (2003). *The landscape of qualitative research: Theories and issues.* (2nd ed.) Thousand Oaks, CA: Sage.

Drake, D. (2005). Creating third space: The use of narrative liminality in coaching. In I. F. Stein, F. Campone, & L. J. Page (Eds.), *Proceedings of the Second International Coaching Federation Coaching Research Symposium* (pp. 50-59). Washington, DC: International Coach Federation.

Edwards, J. (2005). The process of becoming and helping others to become: A grounded theory study. In I. F. Stein, F. Campone, & L. J. Page (Eds.), *Proceedings of the Second International Coaching Federation Coaching Research Symposium* (pp. 69-78). Washington, DC: International Coach Federation.

Grant, A. (2004). Keeping up with the cheese: Research as a foundation for professional coaching of the future. In I. F. Stein, & L. A. Beltsen (Eds.), *Proceedings of the First International Coaching Federation Coaching Research Symposium* (pp. 1-19). Mooresville, NC: Paw Print Press.

Hurd, J. (2004). Learning for life: An investigation into the effect of organizational coaching on individual lives. In I. F. Stein & L. A. Beltsen (Eds.), *Proceedings of the First International Coaching Federation Coaching Research Symposium* (pp. 33-42). Mooresville, NC: Paw Print Press.

Laske, O., Stober, D., & Edwards, J. (2005) Whitepaper: What is, and why should we care about, evidence-based coaching? In I. F. Stein, F. Campone, & L. J. Page (Eds.), *Proceedings of the Second International Coaching Federation Coaching Research Symposium* (pp. 169-174. Washington, DC: International Coach Federation.

Lew, S., Wolfred, T., Gislason, M., & Con, D. L. (2004) Executive coaching project: Evaluation of findings. In I. F. Stein & L. A. Beltsen (Eds.), *Proceedings of the First International Coaching Federation Coaching Research Symposium* (pp. 62-69). Mooresville, NC: Paw Print Press.

Maxwell, J. (2005). Qualitative Research design: An interactive approach. (2nd ed.) *Applied Social Research Methods Series, 41.* Thousand Oaks, CA: Sage.

McCready, L. (2005). Coaching for employee engagement at Manpower. In I.F. Stein, F. Campone, & L. J. Page (Eds.), *Proceedings of the Second International Coaching Federation Coaching Research Symposium* (pp. 95-102). Washington, DC: International Coach Federation.

Pearce, B. (in press). Dialogue for coaching research: Education, practice and more research. In F. Campone & J. L. Bennett (Eds.), *Proceedings of the Third International Coaching Federation Coaching Research Symposium.* Lexington, KY: International Coach Federation.

Robson, C. (2002). *Real world research.* (2nd ed.) Malden, MA: Blackwell

Schön, D. (1983). *The reflective practitioner: How professionals think in action.* New York, NY: Basic Books

Severin, C. S. (2004). ROI in executive coaching: Using total factor productivity. In I. F. Stein & L. A. Beltsen (Eds.), *Proceedings of the First International Coaching Federation Coaching Research Symposium* (pp. 141-142). Mooresville, NC: Paw Print Press

Stober, D. (2005) Coaching eye for the research guy and research eye for the coaching guy: 20/20 vision for coaching through the scientist-practitioner model. In I. F. Stein, F. Campone, & L. F. Page (Eds.), *Proceedings of the Second International Coaching Federation Coaching Research Symposium* (pp. 13-21). Washington, DC: International Coach Federation.

[1] Put simply, Heisenberg demonstrated that someone observing an object in motion, a tennis ball for example, could either measure the location of the ball in space or the speed at which it is traveling but not both simultaneously. A second facet of Heisenberg's experiments demonstrated that the object of study (in his case an electron traveling through space), could manifest as a particle or a wave. The experimenter's choice of focus collapsed the multiple possible states into one through the act of observation. I am indebted to my physicist husband, Ed Spargo, Ph.D., for his help in distilling Heisenberg into a footnote.

Francine Campone, Ed.D., PCC served as a university counselor, faculty member and Associate Dean of Students over the course of a twenty-nine year career. She earned her doctorate in Higher and Adult Education from Columbia University. She earned the International Coach Federation's Professional Certified Coach (PCC) designation. Training in humanistic mediation, group dynamics and facilitation, and Constructive Living Practice complements her coach training. Francine works extensively with leaders of education and nonprofit organizations, and with individuals and teams facing in significant transitions. A founding faculty member of the School of Management's graduate coaching certification program at the University of Texas at Dallas, Francine developed and teaches a course in research for coaches. Dr. Campone was co-editor of the Proceedings of the 2004 ICF Research Symposium and is a member of the leadership team for the 2005 Symposium as well as co-editor of this year's Proceedings. Contact: fcampone@rushmore.com.